MW00416899

THE HISTORY OF
Penn
TREATY PARK

Fairman's Mansion and Treaty Tree, engraved by John Serz after Brittan, published by J. Quig in Philadelphia, circa 1840–50. *Courtesy John Connors Collection.*

THE HISTORY OF Penn TREATY PARK

KENNETH W. MILANO

Published by The History Press
Charleston, SC 29403
www.historypress.net

Cover design by Natasha Momberger

First published 2009
Second printing 2009

Manufactured in the United States

ISBN 978.1.59629.488.2

Library of Congress Cataloging-in-Publication Data

Milano, Kenneth W.
The history of Penn Treaty Park / Kenneth W. Milano.
p. cm.
ISBN 978-1-59629-488-2
1. Penn Treaty Park (Philadelphia, Pa.)--History. 2. Parks--Pennsylvania--Philadelphia--History. 3. Penn's Treaty with the Indians (1682)--History. 4. Penn's Treaty with the Indians (1682)--In art. 5. Penn, William, 1644-1718--Relations with Indians. 6. Philadelphia (Pa.)--History. 7. Philadelphia (Pa.)--Description and travel. I. Title.
F158.65.P4M55 2009
974.8'11--dc22
2008043991

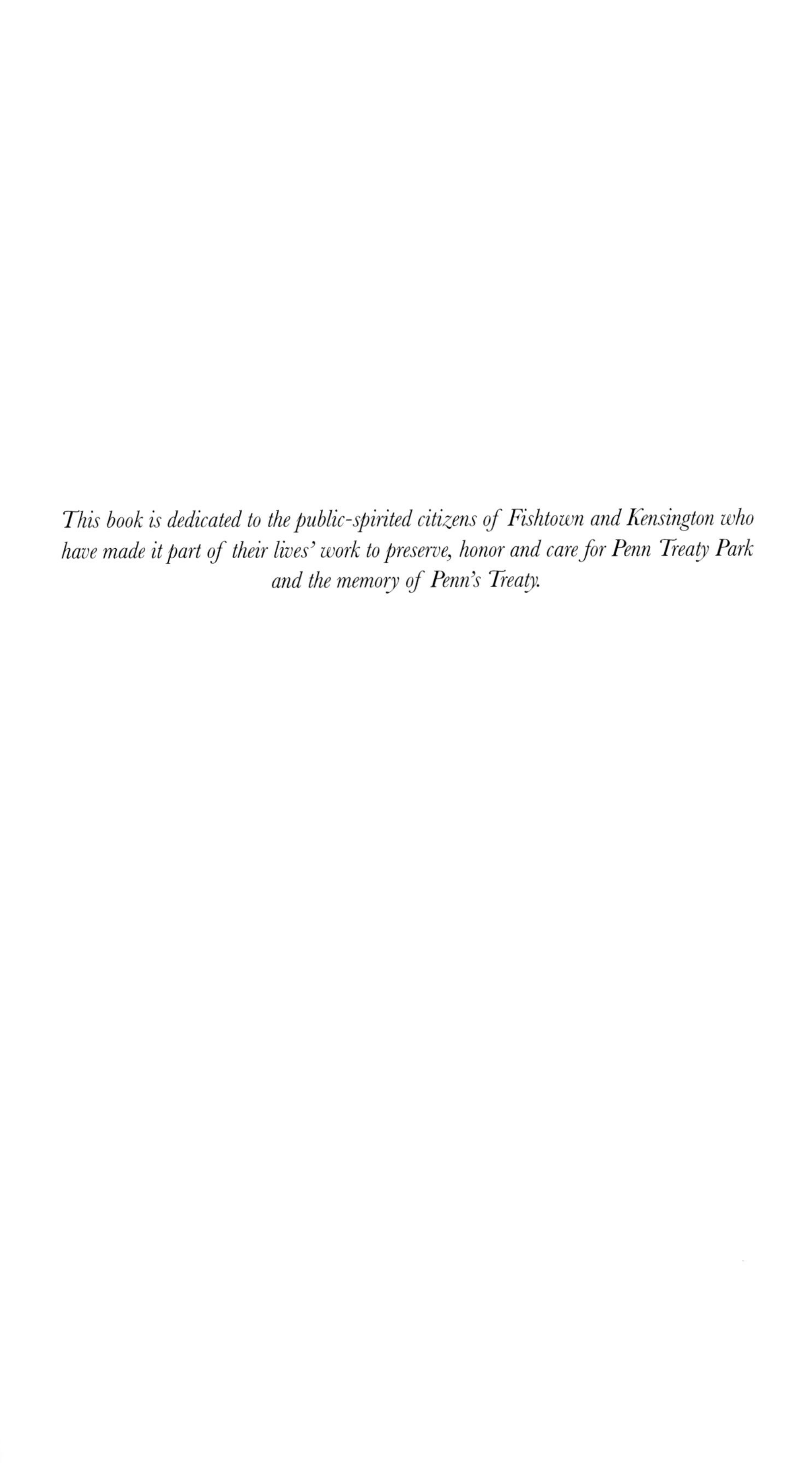

This book is dedicated to the public-spirited citizens of Fishtown and Kensington who have made it part of their lives' work to preserve, honor and care for Penn Treaty Park and the memory of Penn's Treaty.

CONTENTS

FOREWORD

In 1682, along the gentle banks of the Delaware River, under the shade of a great elm tree in an area then known as Shackamaxon, William Penn is believed to have made a Treaty of Amity and Friendship with the Native Americans.

Few events in American history are noted for the just and fair treatment of peoples from different cultures. The legend of William Penn's Treaty with the Indians became a universal symbol of religious and civil liberties. Voltaire made reference to the event in 1764, and artists throughout Europe recreated the scene first painted by Benjamin West in 1771. Drawings of the transaction were used to promote commercial interest in the emerging land. American painter Edward Hicks created numerous depictions of the treaty meeting to promote social change. In the pre–Civil War era, artistic renderings of Penn's Treaty were used to encourage political movements, religious agendas and social reforms.

Most artists rendered Penn, the English Quaker, and the Native Americans as meeting in friendship and trust beneath the branches of a stately elm tree. The "Great Elm," as it was known, remained as a living monument to this event until it fell during a violent storm in 1810. Concerned citizens thought that the site, and perhaps the event itself, would be forgotten once the mighty tree had toppled. Much of the timber was salvaged, however, and many objects were crafted from the tree's wood, ensuring that the significance of this unique event was not lost. The first public monument, an obelisk, was placed on what was then private property to mark the site of the historic tree.

In 1831, Chief Justice John Marshall received a box created from the Treaty Elm from Roberts Vaux. Marshall replied:

> *The box is to me an inestimable relique. I know no inanimate object more entitled to our reverence than the tree of which it was a part, because I think few events in history have stronger claims on our serious reflection, on our humanity, our sense of rights, and on our judgment, than the treaty which was made under it, and the consequences which followed that treaty. The plainly marked difference of intercourse between the colonists of Pennsylvania and the aborigines, and that which other colonists maintained with them, furnishes a practical lesson on the influence which intelligence, real friendship, and justice may acquire and preserves over their untutored minds which ought not even yet to be forgotten.*

Interest in creating a permanent park and preserving the site continued throughout the years. Penn Treaty Park was officially established in 1893. Native Americans have always honored the location of this peaceful event along the river, handing down the story of this historic occurrence in their traditional oral history, and have gathered at the site on numerous occasions in the past 326 years.

This book is inspired in part by Dr. Etta May Pettyjohn (1909–2005), who for many years championed the preservation of Penn Treaty Park and outlined a vision for a museum in 1970. Dr. Pettyjohn was a member of the tercentenary committee and often spoke of how this simple event had an impact on political and social change in the young America. She believed that the story of Penn Treaty Park richly deserved a museum as a permanent tribute to the extraordinary message of Penn's Treaty from long ago.

Today, the Fairmount Park Commission maintains the grounds with oversight from the Friends of Penn Treaty Park.

John Connors, 2008

ACKNOWLEDGEMENTS

A big thanks goes out to John Connors, who made this book possible by initially asking me to write the history of Penn Treaty Park for his website. John loaned me his files, photos and images of the park and Penn's Treaty, and he had his Penn Treaty collection photographed so it could be used in this book. I would also like to thank John for introducing me to the lore of Henry C. Kreiss and Dr. Etta May Pettyjohn, two individuals without whom, I'm sure, the park would never have made it this long.

Also a big thanks to John Connors's team of people who worked on his website and also helped me with this book—in particular Gail Sweet and Carol Smythe, who edited and proofread the original manuscript that I wrote for the website (much of which is incorporated into this book). And to Karen Mauch, who trekked out to Penn Treaty Park on a couple of occasions and snapped some photographs for me. And to Kelli Lucas, who helped with the art and print descriptions of John's collection.

Georgia Holder and Beverly Daugherty of the Daughters of the American Colonists helped to answer questions I had on the DAC's previous president, Mary H. Foster. Elaine "the William Penn Lady" Peden and Dr. Lois Baker, wife of Kensington historian George Baker, were both kind and answered my questions, as well.

Artist Bob Haozous is to be thanked for having one of his representatives call me to answer some questions I had about his Penn Treaty sculpture.

Sandy Salzman's memory helped to answer questions I had about the early years of the Fishtown Civic Association and their involvement in the park's history and the Indian sculpture competition.

Christopher R. Dougherty at the archives of the Fairmount Park Commission was very helpful in unearthing documents, maps and plans of the park's history and answering any questions that I had.

Torben Jenk and Rich Remer of the Kensington History Project are my constant colleagues in researching the histories of Fishtown and Kensington, and they certainly have their fingerprints on this book as well.

Undoubtedly, there are others who contributed to this book, and if I forgot to mention you by name, be it known that you are thanked!

Any faults or errors belong to the author.

INTRODUCTION

The Lenni-Lenapes, or Delaware Indians

Along the creeks and streams that traversed the Middle Atlantic States, and in particular the Delaware River, lived the Lenni-Lenapes, a group of Algonquian-speaking Native Americans. From northern Delaware to southeastern New York, and from the Atlantic Ocean to the forests of eastern Pennsylvania, the Lenni-Lenapes made their homes.

The Lenapes are also known as the Delaware Indians. They acquired this name from the English colonists of the Delaware River Valley. Captain Samuel Argall is credited as the first European to discover a large bay of water in the year 1610. Argall named this body the Delaware Bay in honor of Sir Thomas West, Third Lord de la Warr, who at that time was the governor of the colony of Virginia. The name Delaware was then used for the river that fed the bay and given to the Lenni-Lenape Indians who inhabited the Delaware Valley.

The Lenni-Lenapes were not one single tribe but rather were made up of three groups. In the northern areas of Lenape territory were the Munsees, "the people of the stoney country." In the middle or central area, where Philadelphia came to be located, were the Unamis, or the "people downriver." South of the Unamis were the Unalactgios, or the "people near the ocean," who were also known as the Nanticokes.

The Unami tribe is the group that lived at Shackamaxon, this location being just one of the settlements that they occupied, but apparently one of the more important. The full boundaries of the Unami homeland were the northern two-thirds of New Jersey (including what would become New York's Staten Island) and the adjoining parts of eastern Pennsylvania woodland, down to just below the future city of Philadelphia.

Besides the three territorial groups (with their three dialects) that made up the Lenni-Lenapes, there were also three different matrilineal clans that were present in the groups: the Turtle, Wolf and Turkey Clans. The Turtle Clan was the most important, and usually the sachem, or chief of the tribal councils, was from this clan. Tamanend, the head sachem who made the Peace Treaty with William Penn, was from the Turtle Clan of the Unamis and would have been the one who ruled the area of Shackamaxon.

The settlements of the Lenapes were described as a "series of small autonomous communities situated on navigable streams" on each side of the Delaware River, each with its "own town chief, or king, and his great men." A settlement typically had a rectangular council house and various kinds of wigwams.

The villages of the Lenapes were often occupied by several hundred people in the summer months and fewer in the winter months, as many of the men departed for the interior to hunt. They used dugout canoes for transportation, and at Shackamaxon there was a canoe ferry across the Delaware River to New Jersey. Much of their diet was sustained by farming, and it was not uncommon to see a farm of two hundred acres.

By the seventeenth century, the Lenapes were decimated by warfare with other Native American tribes over the trade with the Europeans and by epidemics brought by the Europeans, as well. The Lenni-Lenapes were only a remnant of a larger and greater people when William Penn arrived in 1682 to make his treaty of peace.

Shackamaxon, the setting of Penn's Treaty, was a special place for the Unamis, the Lenapes and their neighboring tribes. They would gather here in the summer months to fish, retreating into the woods to hunt when winter came, and to cross over the Delaware to New Jersey. It was also considered a neutral ground, where "representatives of all the tribes on fresh water and east of the Alleghenies between the Potomac, the Hudson, and the lakes, the Iroquois, the Nanticokes, the Susquehannocks, and the Shawanees—were accustomed to kindle their council fires, smoke the pipe of deliberations, [and] exchange the wampum belts of explanation and treaty." It is no wonder, then, that it was at Shackamaxon where William Penn made his Peace Treaty with the Lenni-Lenapes.

WILLIAM PENN

William Penn (1644–1718) was born in London, England, the first child of Vice-Admiral Sir William Penn (circa 1621–1670) and Margaret Jasper, the daughter of a well-to-do Rotterdam merchant. Admiral Penn owed his advancement and appointment to Oliver Cromwell, but when he thought the times were ripe he betrayed the Lord Protector and offered his fleet to Charles II, thus becoming a great favorite with Charles and the Duke of York (the latter became Penn's son's protector for "the father's sake").

While young and still in grammar school, William Penn had visions similar to those of George Fox's "Inner Light," though he had never heard of Fox, the founder of Quakerism. Penn was sent from grammar school to Oxford, and he entered Christ Church College at the age of fifteen, where he "studied assiduously" and "joined the serious set." He went

> *to hear Thomas Loe preach the new gospel of the Society of Friends* [Quakers] *and he resented the discipline which the college attempted to put upon him and his intimates and in consequence he was expelled from the university for rejecting the surplice and rioting in the quadrangle.*

As might be expected, the expulsion from Oxford did not sit well with Admiral Penn and it is said that he beat his son. Admiral Penn was very distressed by his son's nonconformity. After Penn's expulsion, his father sent him to France, where "he came home with the manners and dress of a courtier." After France, his father took him to sea "to prove to the court, when he returned as bearer of dispatches, that he was capable of beginning the career of office." Penn's father still wanted to make something of his son at the court of England, to possibly gain a peerage for the family.

Penn's father later sent him to the Duke of Ormond and gave his son charge of his Irish estates at the same time. In Cork, Penn met the Quaker Thomas Loe again, and Penn is said to have heard a sermon on the text "There is a faith which overcomes the world, and there is a faith which is overcome by the world."

It is thought that it was at this meeting with Loe that William Penn became a confirmed Quaker. His father called him back to England but was unable to break his son's Quaker convictions. Penn now joined the Quakers regularly and became the most prominent follower of their gifted leader, George Fox. Penn's admiration for Fox was "deep and strong," and he repeatedly used his influence to help release Fox from jail after he had been arrested a number of times.

Penn resumed his relations with the Duke of York and secured the prince's influence on behalf of the Society of Friends. Penn's alliance with the Duke of York (a closet Catholic) led to William Penn's settlement of Pennsylvania. When Penn returned from his first visit to his colony, he resumed his place at court upon the accession of James II (the former Duke of York) as one of the most considerable men in the kingdom. He had the monarch's private ear and was able to use his influence on the side of justice and humanity.

WILLIAM PENN ACQUIRES HIS CHARTER FOR PENNSYLVANIA

When Admiral Penn died in 1670, he left his son William property amounting to £1,500 a year in English and Irish estate rents. There was also a claim against the government of King Charles for money lent, which with interest amounted to £15,000. The king had no money and no credit; with William Penn he now resolved to establish a colony in America and remove there with his family so as to be at the head of a new Quaker community and commonwealth. Penn petitioned the king to grant him land in the New World in exchange for the claim of £15,000. Penn asked for "a tract of country in America north of Maryland, with the Delaware on its east, its western limits the same as those of Maryland, and its northern boundary as far as plantable country extended."

Penn's petition was received June 14, 1680. His objective was not only to provide a peaceful home for persecuted members of the Society of Friends, but also to afford asylum for the oppressed Christians of the world.

The petition encountered much opposition. There was strong resistance in the privy council to the idea of someone like Penn being permitted to establish a colony after his own design. His theories of government were thought to be "Utopian and dangerous to Church and State." However, he had powerful friends in the Earl of Sunderland, Lord Hyde, Chief Justice North, the Earl of Halifax and the Duke of York. He had an interview with the Duke of York and was able to win him over to look upon his project in affirmation. Penn's petition for a land grant in America was approved.

King Charles made a public proclamation on Penn's patent that was addressed mainly to the inhabitants of the territory, asking them to yield obedience to Penn and his officials. At the same time, Penn also addressed a letter to the inhabitants of the province, wishing them all happiness and telling them that they were not now at the mercy of a governor looking to make a fortune, writing, "You shall be governed by laws of your own making, and live a free and, if you will, a sober and industrious people. I shall not usurp the right of any or oppress his person. God has furnished me with a better resolution and has given me his grace to keep it."

William Penn's deputy for his new colony and the person to act on his behalf until he arrived was his cousin, William Markham, a captain in the British army. He was commissioned in April 1681 to go out to Pennsylvania and act in that capacity until Penn's arrival. In the same month, Penn sent out Captain Thomas Holme to act as surveyor general of Pennsylvania, and in May Penn published his *Frame of Government.* By June, Penn had sold 565,500 acres of land in the new province, in parcels from 250 to 20,000 acres in size.

In October, Penn sent out three commissioners—William Crispin, John Bezar and Nathaniel Allen—to cooperate with Markham in selecting and laying out a site for Penn's proposed great city. They were also given very full, careful and explicit instructions by Penn, particularly for dealing with the Indians, as some Indian titles needed to be extinguished by them. He wrote a letter to the Indians themselves via these commissioners, which shows that he had studied the Native American character very carefully. It touched the Indians' faith in the one universal Great Spirit and finely appealed to their strong, innate sense of justice. Penn did not wish "to enjoy the great province his king had given him," he said, "without the Indians' consent."

The American Indians had suffered greatly from other Europeans, but Penn assured them that

> *I am not such a man* [self-seeker] *as is well known in my own country, I have a great love and regard for you, and I desire to win and gain your love and friendship by a kind, just, and peaceable life, and the people I send are all of the same mind, and shall in all things behave themselves accordingly, and if in anything any shall offend you or your people, you shall have a full and speedy satisfaction for the same by an equal number of just men on both sides, that by no means you may have just occasion of being offended against them.*

This was the initial step in that "traditional policy" of Penn and the Quakers toward the Indians that was maintained for many years afterward.

On September 1, 1682, William Penn was ready to sail on the ship *Welcome* for Pennsylvania and the New World.

SHACKAMAXON—WORKING HEADQUARTERS OF PENN'S NEW COLONY

At the time of Penn's arrival to his colony, Shackamaxon had long been a fishing and meeting place of the Lenni-Lenapes and had also become a scattered farming settlement for six Swedish families. The area of Shackamaxon would eventually evolve into the Philadelphia neighborhoods of Kensington, Fishtown and Port Richmond. The area sits on the Delaware River about a mile north of the future site of Penn's Philadelphia. Upon the arrival of the English, the Swedes soon sold their land and moved farther into the interior, upriver or across the Delaware River to New Jersey.

Thomas Fairman, an early settler in Burlington, New Jersey, married Elizabeth Kinsey, who previous to her marriage had purchased three hundred acres in the Delaware Valley from Lasse Cock, an original Swedish settler who was Penn's interpreter at the Peace Treaty. Elizabeth Kinsey had completed a land transaction in 1678 that was previously initiated by her father. John Kinsey, one of the founders of Burlington, New Jersey, and a commissioner for West Jersey, died in 1677 before the land deal was completed.

After marrying Kinsey in December 1680, Thomas Fairman moved to Shackamaxon and possibly lived in a home already built by the Swedes. Fairman would eventually build a larger brick dwelling that would come to be known as Fairman's Mansion. This stately house was depicted in Benjamin West's famous painting of Penn's Treaty but was, in fact, not yet constructed of brick at the time of the Peace Treaty.

Thomas Fairman was known as a good surveyor. When Penn acquired his colony of Pennsylvania in 1681, Fairman was hired to assist Penn's surveyor general, Thomas Holme. Fairman had been in the Delaware Valley for several years before Penn's arrival. Compared to Penn's people, Fairman was more familiar with the local geography and inhabitants, including the Swedish settlers who owned the land where Penn wanted to build his city. Fairman was appointed to negotiate the purchase of the land that was owned by the Swanson family for the location of the city of Philadelphia.

Shackamaxon became the gathering place for many of William Penn's major officials, including William Penn himself, upon their arrival to the Pennsylvania colony. When Thomas Holme, assistant to the deputy governor and surveyor general of the province, first arrived at the Pennsylvania colony, William Markham (Penn's cousin and the deputy governor of the colony), or one of his people, directed Holme to Thomas Fairman's house at Shackamaxon. Markham had already been staying with Fairman. When Thomas Fairman handed in his accounts to William Penn, the accounts included expenses for lodging Markham and Holme.

Fairman assisted Markham and Holme on "various exploratory trips to identify the areas to be surveyed." Upon Holme's arrival, Fairman loaned him horses so that he could "ride into the interior of the land and see what it held," and Fairman often accompanied him on these excursions. After Holme surveyed an area for himself, he had Fairman and several others set aside five hundred acres next to Deputy Governor Markham, adjoining Penn's Pennsbury Manor.

On the other side of Holme's land was William Haige, another of Fairman's boarders at Shackamaxon. Haige was one of four land commissioners appointed by William Penn to help develop the land policies for the establishment of Penn's colony. All of these high officials had their country estates surveyed for them next to each other on the Delaware River, north of the city.

The proprietor of Pennsylvania, William Penn; his deputy governor, William Markham; his surveyor general, Thomas Holme; and his land commissioner, William Haige, were all early residents of Shackamaxon and stayed at Thomas Fairman's home. It is no wonder, then, that the Treaty of Amity and Friendship that Penn would make with the Indians took place at Shackamaxon, as it was effectively the initial working headquarters of Penn's new colony.

At one point, Fairman gave up his Shackamaxon home to William Penn and removed to "near Frankford," where his son William was born in 1683. He was also asked to help establish a Quaker meetinghouse at Frankford. The Society of Friends' Abington Meetinghouse is one of the "earliest congregations dating back to when people gathered at Thomas Fairman's home at Shackamaxon, before the arrival of William Penn."

It was this familiarity with Shackamaxon, the center of activity for Penn and his officials, that would make William Penn venture north from Upland (now Chester), the "official" capital of the colony, in order to treat with the Indians in the now-famous Treaty of Amity and Friendship at Shackamaxon, an accord that helped paved the way for the founding of Penn's colony of Pennsylvania.

CHAPTER I

PENN'S TREATY, BENJAMIN WEST AND HIS FOLLOWERS

Penn's Treaty

William Penn's memorable treaty with Tamanend and other Delaware chiefs under the "Great Elm Tree" at Shackamaxon has always attracted romantic interest. Historian C. Hale Sipe tells us that Penn, unarmed, clad in his somber Quaker garb, addressed the assembled Native Americans, uttering the following words, which have been admired ever since:

> *We meet on the broad pathway of good faith and good-will; no advantage shall be taken on either side, but all shall be openness and love. We are the same as if one man's body was to be divided into two parts; we are of one flesh and one blood.*

The reply of Tamanend is said to be equally noble:

> *We will live in love with William Penn and his children as long as the creeks and rivers run, and while the sun, moon, and stars endure.*

There is no actual record of the "Great Treaty," the treaty made familiar to many by Benjamin West's painting and Voltaire's allusion to it "as the only treaty never sworn to and never broken." The symbolism of the "Treaty

Tree" has laid its mark on the American landscape as centuries of artists have looked to it for inspiration.

The lack of agreement among historians as to the time when the event took place also adds to the confusion of its authenticity. Most accounts claim that it took place in late November 1682, shortly after Penn arrived in the colony. "Under the shelter of the forest," to quote the American historian George Bancroft, "now leafless by the frosts of autumn, Penn proclaimed to the men of the Algonquin race, from both banks of the Delaware, from the borders of the Schuylkill, and…even from the Susquehanna."

Some historians actually place the date of the treaty as June 23, 1683, when Penn purchased two tracts of land from Tamanend and his associates, with the assumption that the transaction and the Great Treaty took place at the same time and place, even though a treaty of "amity and friendship" need not have included an exchange of land.

Historian Howard Malcom Jenkins makes mention of Penn's Treaty in his multivolume work on Pennsylvania, *Pennsylvania, Colonial and Federal*, published in 1903:

> *The Indians preserved the tradition of an agreement of peace made with Penn, and it was many times recalled in the meetings held with him and his successors. Some of these allusions are very definite. In 1715, for example, an important delegation of the Lenape chiefs came to Philadelphia to visit the Governor. Sassoonan—afterward called Allummapees, and for many years the principal chief of his people—was at the head, and Opessah, a Shawnee chief, accompanied him. There was "great ceremony," says the Council record, over the "opening of the calumet." Rattles were shaken, and songs were chanted. Then Sassoonan spoke, offering the calumet to Governor Gookin, who in his speech spoke of "that firm Peace that was settled between William Penn, the founder and chief governor of this country, at his first coming into it," to which Sassoonan replied that they had come "to renew the former bond of friendship; that William Penn had at his first coming made a clear and open road all the way to the Indians, and they desired the same might be kept open and that all obstructions might be removed."*

Mentioning that the peace was first made upon Penn's coming to the colony would place the Peace Treaty in 1682 rather than 1683—would Penn really wait from October 1682 to June 1683 to make a treaty with the Indians?

In 1720, Governor William Keith, writing to the Iroquois chiefs of New York, noted, "When Governor Penn first settled this country he made it his first care to cultivate a strict alliance and friendship with all the Indians, and condescended so far as to purchase his lands from them." And in March 1722, the colonial authorities sent a message to the Senecas, writing, "William Penn made a firm peace and league with the Indians in these parts near forty years ago, which league has often been repeated and never broken." In fact the Great Treaty was never broken until the Penn's Creek Massacre of October 16, 1755.

According to the historian C. Hale Sipe, the Great Treaty was "preserved by the head chiefs of the Turtle Clan of Delawares for generations." On March 24, 1782, Chief Killbuck is said to have lost the historic wampum that contained the treaty that Tamanend and others had made with Penn one hundred years previously. He had been forced to flee to Fort Pitt to escape death at the hands of the Scotch-Irish settlers from Chartiers Creek who attacked him and other friendly Delawares at Smoky Island, also called Killbuck's Island, in the Ohio River near Fort Pitt.

The Great Treaty at Shackamaxon, as Sipe states, occupies a "high and glorious place in the Indian history and traditions of Pennsylvania and the Nation. Though the historian labors in vain to establish the date, the fact of the treaty remains as inspiring to us of the present days as it was to the historians, painters, and poets of the past." For artists around the world, Penn's Treaty became a symbol and an inspiration that would keep them busy for centuries after.

BENJAMIN WEST'S *PENN'S TREATY WITH THE INDIANS AT SHACKAMAXON* AND THE ARTWORK THAT FOLLOWED

Benjamin West (1738–1820) was born in Springfield, Pennsylvania, the son of John West, an innkeeper, and his second wife, Sarah Pearson. While both parents had Quaker backgrounds, Benjamin did not follow their faith. An English artist, William Williams, and a German artist, John Valentine Haidt, encouraged the young West to study painting. West's artwork came to the attention of the Reverend William Smith, provost of the College of Philadelphia (later the University of Pennsylvania). Smith was impressed with West and invited him to live in Philadelphia and get a classical education that would help further West's career.

West moved to Philadelphia about 1756 and attended college for a short time before traveling to Italy in 1760, again with Smith's help. From Italy,

West went to Paris and then to London. He successfully exhibited paintings at the Society of Artists (precursor to the Royal Academy) in London. In 1764, he decided to stay in London and his family soon followed.

West's reputation as an artist expanded, and he became the teacher for several generations of painters, including American artist Wilson Peale, who came to London in the 1760s. Two of America's most famous painters, Gilbert Stuart and John Trumbull, worked in West's studio as assistants in the 1770s and 1780s, as did West's two sons, who assisted their father in later years.

West made his reputation as a painter of history and became the "leading exponent of neoclassicism in England." At this time, he helped found the Royal Academy, which was established by royal commission in 1768. West later became its second president and served for twenty-seven years, the longest of any president. To support a "distinguished national school of painting," King George III commissioned about sixty paintings. In 1772, West became the "History Painter to the King," which lasted until 1801, when the decline in health of George III, his patron, dried up his royal commissions. He continued, however, to receive a royal stipend of £1,000 per year until 1811.

Benjamin West died on March 10, 1820, almost exactly ten years to the day that the Treaty Tree was uprooted in a storm.

At about the time West was made "History Painter to the King," he painted a depiction of the death of General James Wolfe during the English victory over the French at Quebec in 1759. In this painting, West depicted the characters in modern dress. This caused a stir in art circles, as "historic painting" was to be *historic* and not modern. It was also about this time (1771–72) that Benjamin West executed one of his most famous paintings, *Penn's Treaty with the Indians at Shackamaxon.* He also depicted the characters in this work in the then-modern dress. West took great liberties in order to make the painting an "epic."

Benjamin West's interest and knowledge of Penn's Treaty would have come from a background that included his birth in Pennsylvania, the religious background of his Quaker parents and the fact that his mother's father was a friend of William Penn. West also had the opportunity as a youth to gain some knowledge of the local Native Americans—it is alleged that when a party of Indians came to Springfield and saw West's sketches of birds and flowers, the Indians supposedly taught him how to prepare the red and yellow colors that they used to paint their ornaments.

West's painting of Penn's Treaty was commissioned in 1770 or 1771 by William Penn's son, Thomas Penn, and completed sometime in 1771–

Reproduction of *Penn's Treaty with the Indians*, by Benjamin West, 1771–72, which inspired many imitations of this popular image. *Courtesy John Connors Collection.*

72. Little did West know that his painting of Penn's Treaty would begin a centuries-long fascination with the subject. Some say that Thomas Penn commissioned the painting as a way to try to "restore favor" with Pennsylvanians by using his father's "popular image as a man of peace" to support Thomas Penn's interests in Pennsylvania. His reputation had been previously tarnished by the supposed "greed and treachery" he showed in dealing with the American Indians. He had inherited a share in Pennsylvania, along with his brothers John and Richard, on the death of their father in 1718. Thomas left the Quakers and joined the Church of England. This proved to be one of a number of actions that brought him into confrontation with Quaker-dominated Pennsylvania. He also fought the Pennsylvania Assembly's efforts to tax his land and made great efforts to collect back rents due to his family.

In order to stem the alleged criticism of his fellow citizens, Thomas Penn needed to do more than commission a painting, so he commissioned English publisher John Boydell (1719–1804), who was well known for his reproductions of engravings, to come up with an engraving of the Penn Treaty painting. In 1773, Boydell began to advertise his plan to issue a print of Penn's Treaty, copied from the West painting. During the next few years, John Hall, working for Boydell, engraved the plate for the print. The print was published in London in 1775 with the title *William Penn's Treaty with the Indians when he founded the Province of Pennsylvania in North America, 1681.*

In Hall's engraving, the image was reversed from West's painting. The original copper plate was continuously used to reproduce the print as late as 1932.

By publishing this engraving of Penn's Treaty, the image reached a wider audience. The engraving was sent to America, where it sold well and proved a success. Many other artists copied it thereafter. Through West's painting of Penn's Treaty and Boydell's print of West's painting, the Treaty Tree itself also became a popular subject for artists not only in North America but in Continental Europe as well.

The same Boydell print was copied in a smaller version by French printmaker Robert Delaunay (1749–1814), measuring only twelve by twelve inches, with the figures rearranged and compressed, and titled *Guillaume Penn Traite avec les Indiens.* This print appeared around 1778. It was featured as the frontispiece in *Atlas Ameriquain Septentrionale*, an atlas of North America. The scene was executed by a number of other European artists, including French printmaker Jean-Michel Moreau le Jeune (1741–1814) in 1780. A German artist working in Paris copied the Moreau le Jeune print in 1789 and reproduced it in *Histoire Philosophique du Commerce des Indes.* James Charles Armytage (circa 1820–1897), an English engraver, also published the same scene in a book and thus began the generations of reproductions of West's famous painting.

In 1791, the American painter Edward Savage (1761–1817), who painted President Washington, went to London to further his study of art. Part of his studies included copying several of Benjamin West's paintings, including his Peace Treaty painting. By 1794, Savage was back in America; in 1795, he was in Philadelphia exhibiting some of his work. Another version of Penn's Treaty was painted about 1798 by Jacob Whitman.

John James Barralet (1747–1815), a watercolorist of French descent, was born in Ireland. He arrived in Philadelphia from England in 1795. A year later, he painted one of his most famous works, *A View of Philadelphia from the Great Elm Tree in Kensington* (1796). This painting was completed several years before William Birch published his volume of engravings (1798–1800).

William Russell Birch (1755–1834) was born in Warwickshire, England. He eventually went on to study enamel painting. He became quite successful at this and learned the art of engraving as well. He counted the British

The City & Port of Philadelphia, on the River Delaware from Kensington, by William Russell Birch, Philadelphia, 1800, hand-colored copper plate engraving. *Courtesy John Connors Collection.*

painter Sir Joshua Reynolds as a friend and mentor. He was encouraged to move to America.

In 1794, preceding Barralet, Birch immigrated to Philadelphia with his family, which included his equally talented son, Thomas Birch (1779–1851). William Birch carried a letter of introduction from none other than Benjamin West and addressed to William Bingham. This helped Birch to move easily into the "affluent and sophisticated segment of Philadelphia society," which enabled him to find patrons for his artwork.

Birch's best-known work is *The City of Philadelphia in the State of Pennsylvania as it Appeared in 1800.* He was assisted by his son Thomas and an engraver named Samuel Seymour, possibly an English engraver who worked between the years 1819 and 1824 as a landscape painter on *Major Stephen H. Long's Expedition through Arkansas Territory, the Platte River, and the Front Wall of the Rockies.* This collection of Philadelphia views by Birch and company, when published in 1800, offered the

Great Elm Tree of Shackamaxon (now Kensington), painted and engraved by George Lehman, published by William Smith, Philadelphia, circa 1829. *Courtesy John Connors Collection.*

Philadelphia, viewed from Kensington, showing the Treaty Elm, engraved by Davenport. Published by Thomas Kelly, London, circa 1830s, uncolored (as issued) engraving. *Courtesy John Connors Collection.*

first series of views of any American city…The prints provide a unique visual record of Philadelphia at a time when it was the most important and cosmopolitan city in the Western Hemisphere, and for a time was the capital of the newly formed United States.

The fact that Philadelphia was considered one of the most important and cosmopolitan cities in the Western Hemisphere is precisely why people like Birch and Barralet were immigrating to the city. The city also produced England's most famous painter of the day, Benjamin West. Birch's view of Philadelphia proved very popular, and a second edition was published in 1804, a third in 1809 and a fourth in 1827–28. This work of Birch's included as its frontispiece the famous engraving titled *Penn's Tree, with the City & Port of Philadelphia, on the River Delaware from Kensington.* In this print, very similar to Barralet's, Birch took the spotlight off of William Penn and the Indians and put it upon the Treaty Tree itself. This focus on the image of the tree would be repeated over and over by other engravers, printmakers and artists for the rest of the nineteenth and twentieth centuries and into the present.

Edward Hicks, Folk Artist of Penn's Treaty and *Peaceable Kingdom*

Shortly after West, Savage, Barralet and Birch, and after the more popular forms of art that followed them in the first decades of the nineteenth century—art that brought to the eyes of many Americans and Europeans Penn's Treaty of Amity and Friendship—one Bucks County, Pennsylvania artist was going about his work in his own quiet way.

Edward Hicks (1780–1849), later considered by many to be one of America's leading folk artists, was born in 1780 in Langhorne, Bucks County, Pennsylvania. At the age of thirteen, he was apprenticed to a coach maker, where he displayed a talent for painting and soon became a partner in the business. He married in 1803 and eventually had a family of five children. He moved to Newtown, Pennsylvania, and in 1812, having been a devout Quaker his whole life, became a Quaker preacher. His devotion to the Quaker faith led him to leave his job as a decorative carriage painter. He changed his medium and focused "primarily [on] themes of a religious or highly moral nature," which he thought would be more compatible to his Quakerism.

Around 1820 or 1821, it is not known for sure, Hicks became fascinated with the prophecy of Isaiah (Isaiah 11:6–9): "The wolf also shall dwell with the lamb, and the leopard shall lie down with the kid...and a little child shall lead them." This prophecy as "interpreted by Christianity" is "a prophecy of the coming of Christ and the arrival of a peaceful world, in which all animals and human beings live in harmony and prosperity." Hicks began a series of paintings on this topic that came to be titled *The Peaceable Kingdom.* He produced more than sixty versions of this painting and continued to paint this subject for the rest of his life. The last one was completed the day before he died.

Hicks's paintings followed Isaiah's prophecy "closely in its details," and many vignettes that are described in the biblical passage are shown in his paintings. Over the course of the many versions of the subject, such scenes were continually worked into the paintings.

The influences on *The Peaceable Kingdom* came from various sources, but the most predominant origin appears to have come from the John Hall engraving of Benjamin West's *Peace Treaty with the Indians*, which appears in almost every one in the series of paintings that Hicks created. For Hicks, the Peace Treaty symbolized the "Quaker attributes of peace and brotherly

Edward Hicks was inspired to paint over one hundred paintings on Penn's meeting with the Indians, a *Peaceable Kingdom* on earth. *Courtesy John Connors Collection.*

love." Most versions of the painting show an open wilderness, usually with several children surrounded by animals, arranged in the biblical vignettes; somewhere, perhaps in the background or foreground, stood figures of men resembling the popular images of Penn's Treaty with the Indians.

Hicks's religious background, his devotion to the Bible and his love of animals and children seemed to be the major influences that held him to this subject. It is said that "because Hicks knew no other profitable trade and since Quaker ministers were not permitted salaries, he needed the income from his painting to support his large family. The Peaceable Kingdom, as a religious subject and a kind of visual sermon, perhaps helped Hicks to justify his vocation." In addition to the *Peaceable Kingdom* series, Hicks also painted some historic subjects, including several versions of Penn's Treaty with the Indians.

THE FOLLOWERS OF WEST, BIRCH AND HICKS

After West, Birch and Hicks, many subsequent artists have followed with their own ideas and often-unique interpretations of Penn's Treaty with the Indians, some emphasizing the Peace Treaty, others the Treaty Tree.

English engraver George Cooke's (1781–1834) engraving after William Birch, *Philadelphia From the Great Tree, Kensington* (London, May 1812), was widely popular and made available across Europe, and it was soon copied about 1827 by a German artist named J. During and titled *Philadelphia von dem grossen Baum zu Kingston.*

There was also a full-length mezzotint from a painting by Henry Inman (1801–1846) that was published by J. Earle of Philadelphia showing William Penn standing under a tree in the foreground with a scroll in one hand; in the background stood some Indians. The firm of Childs and Inman produced many prints from Inman's portraits.

When Inman decided to leave Childs and Inman, he was replaced by a fellow employee of the firm, George Lehman, a landscape painter, engraver and lithographer from Lancaster County, Pennsylvania. The firm became Childs & Lehman until Childs sold his share to Peter S. Duval and the firm became Lehman & Duval. Lehman stayed with the firm until 1837. Before joining Childs's firm, Lehman had produced a number of artworks, one of which was an 1827 aquatint titled *Under which William Penn concluded his treaty with the Indians in 1682 it fell during a storm in 1810.*

Thomas Birch (1779–1851), William Birch's son, created a later print of *Philadelphia From Kensington* in 1830. Other nineteenth-century artists who

Penn's Treaty with the Indians, rare American historic chintz panel, circa eighteenth century, most likely used as drapery or upholstery. *Courtesy John Connors Collection.*

Guillaume Penn Traite avec les Indiens Etablisant la Province de Pensilvanie dans L'Amerique septentrionale en 1681, engraved by Robert Delaunay, Paris, late eighteenth century. *Courtesy John Connors Collection.*

Guglielmo Penn, alla fondazione di Filadelfia, published by Antonio Fortunato Stella, Milan, Italy, 1827, hand-colored aquatint from Giulio Ferario's *Il Costume Antico e Moderno. Courtesy John Connors Collection.*

Lithophane *William Penn's Treaty with the Indians*, German, circa 1850, cast negative relief, porcelain paste. *Courtesy John Connors Collection.*

worked on the Treaty Tree image included Xanthus Smith (1829–1929), Russell Smith (1812–1896), Harris Steidler, Max Rosenthal and J. Bannister.

These post-1860s renditions of the Penn's Treaty painting and prints may have been influenced by the fact that Joseph Harrison purchased at an English auction Benjamin West's painting of Penn's Treaty. He brought it to Philadelphia, where it was shown privately at his Rittenhouse Square home and publicly until Harrison's death in 1874, when it was given in joint custody to the Pennsylvania Academy of the Fine Arts and the United States National Museum of Independence. The painting was shown in 1864 at the "Great Central Fair" in Logan Square, held by the United States Sanitary Commission to raise money during the Civil War. *Penn's Treaty* was shown in the art gallery of the fair and copies were made and sold at the fair. Today Benjamin West's original painting of Penn's Treaty hangs on the walls of the Pennsylvania Academy of Fine Arts in Philadelphia.

Besides the artists, painters, engravers and printers, the image of the Peace Treaty also appeared in other mediums at this time, including trade cards, posters, calendars, textiles, ceramics, jigsaw puzzles and a host of other mediums. Even the statue of Penn that was placed on the top of

Postcard of Penn's Treaty printed in Germany for the American Historical Art Publications Company, New York and St. Louis, dated 1903. *Courtesy John Connors Collection.*

Victorian chromolithographic trade cards showing the image of *Penn's Treaty*. Companies wanted to be associated with the image of Penn's "fair play." *Courtesy John Connors Collection.*

Philadelphia's city hall is modeled on this early image of Penn by Benjamin West—a scroll in one hand, the other in an outward mode just like West's painting. The statue was also placed so that Penn was facing Kensington, originally Shackamaxon, the scene of his Treaty of Amity and Friendship with the American Indians.

The Pennsylvania State Capitol in Harrisburg and the United States Capitol Building at Washington, D.C., both have depictions of Penn's Treaty.

By the late nineteenth century, the people of Philadelphia finally recognized the need to preserve the place of Penn's Treaty with the Indians once and for all. West's *Penn's Treaty with the Indians*, Birch's prints of *Philadelphia From Kensington* and Hicks's *Peaceable Kingdom*, as well as a host of others that followed them, helped to put Penn's Treaty in the minds of many residents and promote the fact that the treaty did indeed take place at Shackamaxon and that it was most assuredly worth preserving.

CHAPTER 2

THE FALL OF THE TREATY ELM, ELM TREE RELICS, THE PENN SOCIETY AND THE TREATY MONUMENT

In the years following Penn's Treaty at Shackamaxon, the area around Shackamaxon began to slowly develop. In 1729, Anthony Palmer purchased the old Fairman's Mansion and founded his town of Kensington on the surrounding 191½ acres of land. Palmer's development proved successful as many shipwrights welcomed the opportunity to move from the crowded and expensive shorefront of Philadelphia to the white, sandy beaches of Kensington. Soon after, many German immigrants arrived in the area and set up fishing operations. These families would eventually control the entire catch of the Delaware River from Trenton Falls to Cape May. The families were so influential that the oldest part of Kensington, the area just north of Penn Treaty Park, would eventually become known as Fishtown, and in time, the whole of the eastern part of Kensington would give way to this new name.

The area around the Treaty Tree began to be developed with shipyards, and roads were cut through the open fields. Anthony Palmer died in 1749, and Fairman's Mansion came into the possession of Palmer's daughter Elizabeth and her husband Alexander Allaire. The Allaires sold the mansion house to shipbuilder Joseph Lynn and his wife Sarah Fairman. Sarah Fairman was the daughter of one of the heirs of Thomas Fairman, the man who built the mansion house. The house then went through the hands of Joseph Lynn to Thomas Hopkins, Joseph Ball and, finally, to William Yard, who sold it to Matthew Vandusen.

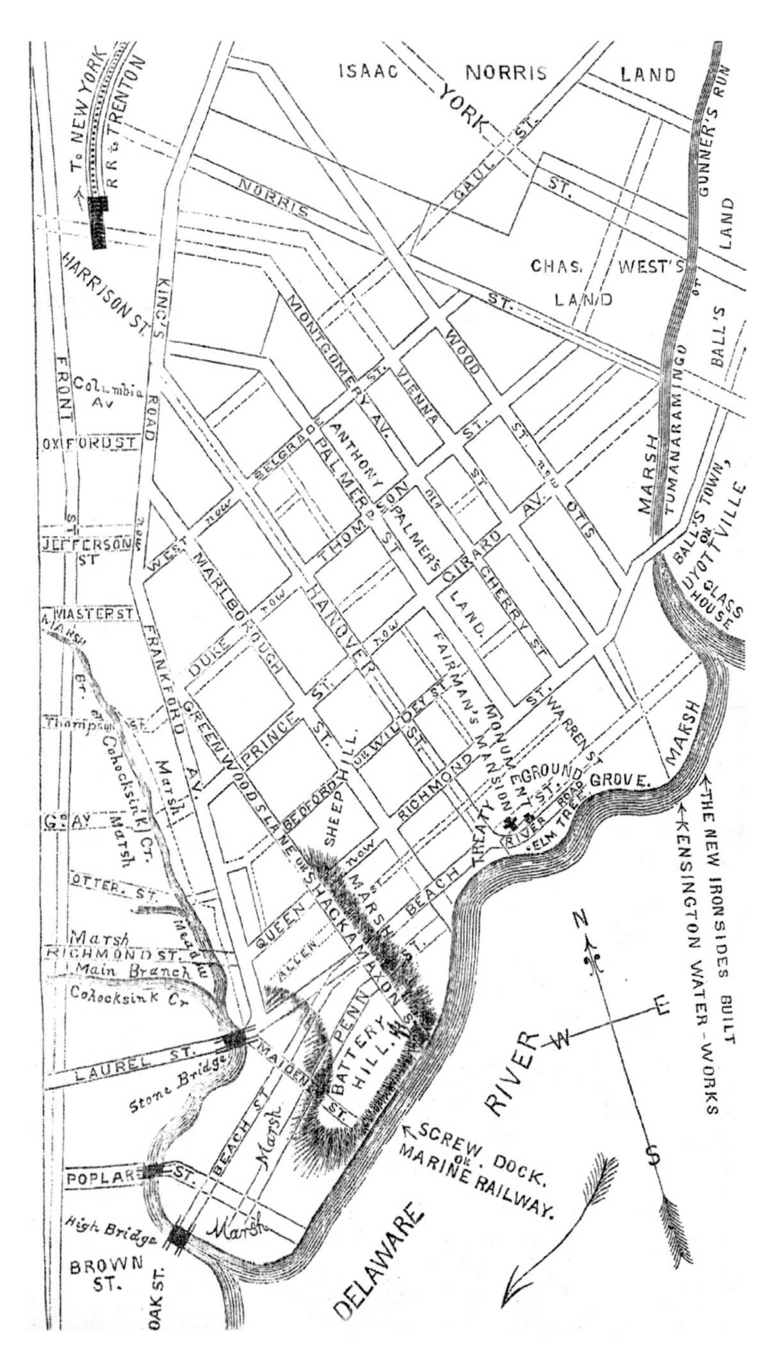

Map showing the distance between the Treaty Elm and General Simcoe's British Redoubt No. 1 (Battery Hill), taken from *Sloan's Architectural Journal & Builder's Review*, 1868. *Courtesy of the author.*

During the American Revolution, the British army occupied Philadelphia from September 1777 to June 1778. The British built their northern fortification lines along roughly what today would be Poplar Street, from the Delaware River on the east to the Schuylkill River on the west. Point Pleasant, an area fewer than two blocks from the Treaty Elm, was the home to British Redoubt No.1, the strongest and most important of the ten British redoubts built along the northern lines. Redoubt No. 1 housed General John Graves Simcoe and the Queen's Rangers, a Loyalist regiment. These soldiers were responsible for helping to make sure the main roads (Frankford and Germantown Roads) into Philadelphia from the northeast and north-central areas of the colony were kept clear of Rebels (Americans) who might try to interfere with the deliveries of foodstuffs meant for the citizens of Philadelphia who stayed behind after the British occupied the city, as well as for the occupying soldiers themselves. The northern suburbs of Philadelphia saw a foraging war carried on by the British and the Americans.

General Simcoe should be given credit for saving the Treaty Elm from being chopped down and used for firewood. It was a cold winter (the winter of "Valley Forge") and many of the trees and orchards in Kensington had already been chopped down by the British to help in the building of their defensive lines, as well as to clear the sightlines in front of their fortifications. General Simcoe, knowing of the history of Penn's Treaty, perhaps from Benjamin West's painting or Hall's engraving, or simply from his knowledge of history, made sure to post guards to care for the Treaty Elm while the British occupied Philadelphia, and thus the Treaty Elm lived through the Revolution.

THE TREATY ELM FALLS

The Fairman's Mansion house and surrounding property, including the lot where the Treaty Elm sat, was purchased by Matthew Vandusen (1759–1812) in 1795. The original 191½ acres that Anthony Palmer had purchased with the mansion house in 1729 had shrunk to fewer than a couple of acres, and Palmer's town of Kensington was rapidly developing. Vandusen and his descendants lived in Fairman's Mansion for thirty years before it was torn down to make way for "progress." After the removal of the mansion house, several smaller homes were built on the site, and members of the Vandusen family continued to live on the property.

On March 8, 1810, Philadelphia's *Poulson's American Daily Advertiser* reported on a massive storm that blew through Philadelphia, uprooting the Treaty Elm:

> *During the tremendous gale of Monday night last, the Great Elm Tree at Kensington, under which, it is said, William Penn, the Founder of Pennsylvania, ratified his first treaty with the Aborigines, was torn up by the roots. This celebrated tree, having stood the blast of more than a century since that memorable event, is at length prostrated to the dust! It had long been used as a land-mark, and handsomely terminated a north-east view of the city and liberties on the Delaware.*

This same news story ran in New York's *Columbian* on March 10, and Salem's *Salem-Gazette* in Massachusetts on March 16. A variant of the story ran in New York's *Evening Post* on March 8, 1810:

> *Philadelphia, March 7. After a blow from the north-east on Monday last, about 11 o'clock at night, the wind suddenly shifted to the west and blew a tremendous gale, accompanied with rain—the wind continued blowing violently the whole night and we fear has done very much damage thro' the country. The chimney of Mr. Kay, hatter in Front-Street was blown down, the weight of which carried the whole of a one story kitchen into the cellar; a ship and brig at Kensington, were torn from their fasts and drove across the river and are ashore in Jersey. A great number of trees in and about the city were blown up by the roots, as was also the large tree at Kensington, under which William Penn, the founder of Pennsylvania, signed his first treaty with the Aborigines. This noted tree having stood the blasts of a hundred or more winters since that event is at last tumble unto dust.*

The *Evening Post* story was repeated in the *New York Spectator* on March 10, as well as in the *Boston Mirror* on March 17. Another Boston paper, the *Boston Gazette*, reported the story on March 19. Two weeks after the storm, the story spread across the country as the whole nation took interest.

On March 20, the story was picked up by the *Connecticut Herald*, the *Republican Star* or *Eastern Shore General Advertiser* (Maryland) and the *Washingtonian* (Virginia), and the following day by two other Connecticut papers, the *Courier* and the *Connecticut Gazette*. But the story wasn't dead, yet! On March 24, the *Independent American* in Washington, D.C., ran it, as did the *Vermont Courier* on March 28. By April, the story had circulated as far north as Maine, where reports of the Treaty Tree being blown down were covered in the *Eagle* on April 3 and then again in Vermont's *Weekly Wanderer* on April 6. Finally, by April 28, when the story appeared in Rhode Island's *Columbian Phoenix*, it would appear that the whole country had read that the Treaty Tree was no more.

After the Treaty Tree fell on March 5, 1810, it was revealed that Matthew Vandusen had been warned to brace the Treaty Tree. Over the years, the trunk of the tree had started to lean heavily in a southeasterly fashion, so much so that it was not uncommon to see a goat climbing into the tree. While Vandusen was proud of the tree, he apparently never got around to bracing it, and the winds took it down several days after he received the advice.

The downed tree drew a crowd in the ensuing days as souvenir hunters gathered from near and far. The tree lay on the grown for nearly two years before anything was done with it. During this time, many pieces of the tree were taken away by relic hunters. It is reported that the Kensington Treaty Tree became so valuable and so highly prized by relic hunters that the family found it necessary to have a guard placed about the premises to prevent further destruction. It was finally decided to uproot the rest of the tree, of which the only thing left by this time was about "eight to ten feet of the trunk, or body of the tree attached to the broken stump, the roots remaining in the ground." These pieces were hauled by ten horses to Franklin Eyre's saw shed next door to the Vandusens, where carpenters from Vandusen's shipyard, which occupied the treaty grounds, "whip-sawed their timbers and other lumber for the purpose of sawing it into two-inch plank to be used in making articles as mementos of the great and renowned treaty and tree."

John Eggleston was the person hired to haul the Treaty Elm to Eyre's saw yard, where Eyre kept half of the workable boards with the other half going back to the Vandusen family, in particular to Captain Paul Ambrose Oliver and his wife Mary Vandusen, the daughter of Matthew Vandusen.

RELICS OF THE TREATY TREE

Roberts Vaux—who would later become one of the founders of the Penn Society and one of the first advocates and supporters for the erection of a memorial at the site of Penn's Treaty—appears to have been one of the individuals who, at some point, acquired a large enough piece of the Treaty Tree to have made from it at least eight small boxes, which he sent to various friends and associates.

One of the earliest records of Vaux sending a box is noted in a letter written by T. Cadwalader on January 7, 1821. In the letter, Cadwalader thanks Vaux for the "two boxes made of the root of the celebrated tree under which the wise and illustrious founder of Pennsylvania is said to have made his first Treaty with the native Lords of the Soil." Cadwalader goes on to tell Vaux that he will keep one "as a valued and interesting token" from Vaux, while the other was to be "transmitted to John Penn with a copy of your [Vaux's] letter." T. Cadwalader is probably General Thomas Cadwalader (1779–1841), who distinguished himself in the War of 1812. He also took over the affairs of the Penn family in America in 1817, a task that occupied so much of his time that he retired from his law practice.

In 1822, Vaux wrote to John Binns (1772–1860), offering him a "small box" that was "made of part of the Great Elm" as a

> *humble memorial of a transaction, which was distinguished for its just & pacific character, and associates recollections of a man who breasted persecution in his native land, when tyranny was at its zenith, who tho he was a Quaker, did certainly contribute no small share in asserting, & establishing the civil, & religious freedom, which has enlarged the circle of human happiness.*

An Irish-born Philadelphia journalist and publisher of the *Democratic Press*, John Binns was a liberal reform activist (for which he was imprisoned in the United Kingdom and tried for sedition in 1799). After his release from the gaol in 1801, he immigrated to America. He was one of the first to realize (about 1816) the potential market for a "splendid and correct copy of the Declaration of Independence, with fac-similes of all the signatures."

United States Supreme Court Justice John Marshall was another who received a gift from Roberts Vaux of a small box made from the Treaty Tree. Upon receipt of the box, Marshall had very kind words for Vaux, which are quoted by John Connors in the foreword of this book.

Pennsylvania governor George Wolf (1777–1840) also received a Treaty Tree box from Vaux. Wolf, who was governor of Pennsylvania from 1829 to 1835, wrote a note of thanks and respect dated March 10, 1830:

> *The box itself will be preserved with care and veneration; not only because I esteem it as a precious relict of that mute witness of an important event in the early history of the Commonwealth, by which the foundation of the pacific government of William Penn was laid, but also on account of its highly esteemed and much respected donor.*

Another box made from the Treaty Elm was sent to Hartman Kuhn (1784–1860), who is presumably the Hartman Kuhn who was a trustee of the University of Pennsylvania and one of the members of the original "State Fencibles," a company that was raised by Colonel Clement C. Biddle. He was a merchant and senior member of the firm of Lyle & Newman. In a letter dated June 14, 1832, Kuhn thanked Vaux for the box.

On November 19, 1832, William Wirt (1772–1834), who served as the attorney general for the United States for twelve years, wrote to Vaux thanking him for a Treaty Tree box. Wirt, like Vaux, was a defender of the rights of American Indians. After his term as attorney general, Wirt defended Cherokee rights before the U.S. Supreme Court. Wirt argued in *Cherokee Nation v. Georgia* that "the Cherokee Nation [was] a foreign nation in the sense of our constitution and law" and not subject to Georgia's jurisdiction. While the court did not rule entirely in favor of the Cherokees, it did leave open the possibility that it might rule favorably in the future. Wirt got his chance again in *Worcester v. Georgia*, when the ruling handed down by another Treaty Elm box recipient, Chief Justice John Marshall, stated that in the Cherokee Nation, "the laws of Georgia have no force, and...the citizens of Georgia have no right to enter."

Vaux sent yet another box to the poet and editor Willis Gaylord Clark (1808–1841), who returned his thanks to Vaux in a letter of February 4, 1833. Clark was considered by Edgar Allan Poe to be the "foremost Philadelphia poet of his day." Clark was solicited to manage the *Philadelphia Gazette*, one of the oldest and most respectable journals in Pennsylvania, which he did until his untimely death.

Not to be outdone, Philadelphia annalist and fellow Penn Society founder John Fanning Watson acquired quite a bit of the Treaty Elm as well. Watson stated that he presented to several persons snuffboxes "formed of a plurality of kinds of relic wood," including from the Treaty Tree. He also owned a "lady's work-stand of the Treaty Tree, ornamented with the walnut tree of the Hall of Independence, and some mahogany from Columbus' house." Watson also owned several picture frames whose corners were made from the Treaty Tree.

In his writings, Watson related that a part of the famous tree was "constructed into something memorable and enduring at Penn's Park, in England." He might be referring to a large piece of the Treaty Elm that was sent by Samuel Coates to John Penn, of Stoke Park, England, which "Penn so highly valued as to cause it to be placed on a pedestal in one of the apartments of his mansion and added a brazen tablet to it with a description of its history."

Watson had a particular fascination with the Treaty Elm. He wrote that he

> *had seen another sucker growing on the original spot* [of the Treaty Tree], *a dozen years ago, amid the lumber of the ship yard. It was then about 15 feet high, and might have been still larger but for neglect and abuse. I was aiding to have it boxed in for protection; but, whether from previous barking of the trunk, or from injuring the roots by settling the box it did not long survive the intended kindness.*

In 1836, a notice was published of a gift that Watson presented to the "Town House in Kensington," acknowledging the welcome reception of two elm trees that he planted in the front courtyard of that house as mementos of the Treaty Elm. They were transplanted from the premises once owned by Richard Townsends, where he had erected the first mill in Philadelphia County, later called Roberts' Mill, in Germantown. This "Town House in Kensington" was the District of Kensington's Commissioners' Hall (city hall) during a time when Kensington was a self-governing district. It was located at the northeast corner of Frankford Avenue and Master Street. Later, the Commissioners of Kensington acquired some of the actual Treaty Tree and constructed a"Great Arm Chair of relic wood formed of the real Treaty Tree and sundry other woods designated in a secret drawer attached, so as to perpetuate the facts intended to be consecrated to posterity by the enduring presence of the elegant chair."

Besides the Commissioners' Hall in Kensington, Watson also planted a scion from the Treaty Tree at his home at 122 Price Street in Germantown. Along with the Treaty Tree, he also planted some ivy grown at the William Penn estate in Ireland. A Treaty Tree from the Godfrey farm on Mill Street was also transplanted by Watson to the front of his old home on Main Street, below Shoemaker's Lane, which flourished for some time there before disappearing.

It is not known who gave a Treaty Tree box to President John Quincy Adams—possibly Vaux, Watson or Pierre S. du Ponceau—but Judge Richard Peters observed President Adams using a Treaty Elm box in which to keep his snuff at the second annual Penn Society dinner. In a letter dated November 21, 1825, and sent to Roberts Vaux, Peters related his observation:

> *At the Penn dinner, the President* [U.S.] *took a pinch of snuff out of a very shabby box, said to be made from the wood of the Elm. I was ashamed of the squalidity of the box. I told Mr. Adams, that such a box should only*

be used on a pinch but I would endeavor to prevail on some of our society to have one small more respectful to Penn's memory so that he should not turn up his nose at the box, whatever its contents might titillate him to do. Can such a grave solemn appearance be effected? If all the wood be gone, we are all in a hard box.

Besides Vaux and Watson, many acquired souvenirs of the Great Elm. The eminent Dr. Benjamin Rush had a study chair made out of the Treaty Tree, presented to him in 1811 by Mrs. Pritchett. Samuel Breck, second vice-president for the Historical Society of Pennsylvania, visited the Treaty Elm as it lay in ruins and removed a limb, which he gave to Captain Watson, of the British navy, who promised to present it to the museum in Exeter, England.

Not only had original pieces of the Treaty Tree become collectibles, but later generations and offshoots of the tree were valued as well. On May 17, 1841, J&A Crout, a cabinetmaking business on Sixth Street above Green, had in its inventory a table designed for communion service for one of the local churches, made from the stock of the Penn Treaty Tree that grew in the Pennsylvania Hospital lot. This "Hospital Lot" Treaty Tree was from a

The great-grandson of the original Treaty Elm, which was planted in the park by the Fishtown Civic Association in 1982. *Courtesy Karen Mauch Photography © 2008.*

"shoot" of the original. The same company also manufactured a looking glass frame made from the wood of the original Treaty Elm. This sucker that J&A Crout worked with had been located at the "western vacant lot" of the hospital and was cut down in 1841 when Linden Street was put through. Coates and Brown, managers, had placed it there sometime around 1816.

In October 1842, at an exhibition of American art and manufactures held at the Franklin Institute, there was a large frame on display that was composed of twenty-six different American woods, including a piece of the Treaty Elm that grew in the Pennsylvania Hospital yard on Spruce Street.

On December 29, 1846, workmen assigned to the hospital grounds dug up the remains of the old Penn Treaty Elm. A large number of roots were found, causing some excitement. A number of people again carried off souvenirs.

James E. Murdoch, in January 1864, had constructed an anchor with a chain attached, the crosspiece of the anchor being made from a piece of the Penn Treaty Tree cut off the morning after the old elm was blown down, taken by his father, Lieutenant Thomas Murdoch. The flukes and shaft of the anchor were from the keel of the old *Alliance*, one of John Paul Jones's vessels that had been moored at Petty's Island and had fallen into disrepair and was abandoned.

At the Navy Department Library in Washington, D.C., there is said to be a "fragment of the Penn Treaty Tree." It came into its possession sometime prior to February 1911.

There is also a cup made from the Treaty Tree that found its way into the collection of museum objects of the Massachusetts Historical Society. The cup, along with other objects and manuscripts of the Lamb family, were given to the society in 1969–70 by Misses Aimee and Rosamond Lamb. The Treaty Tree cup is said to have manuscript documentation and provenance to go with it.

One Treaty Tree box went up for auction in California in 2004 and was described as an "Elm wooden box of tongue-and-groove construction with a brass hinge, 4" x 2" x 1 1/8", with beautiful red-rose toning and deep wood grain lines showing." The box included this note in ink on the underside of the lid: "1841 H.S. Gardiner This Box." An accompanying note written by Gardiner states:

> *The Tree was held in high veneration by our Citizens and when it fell as many as could get a piece of it which being made into small Boxes Cups &C. and sent by many to their friends in a far distant Country as a relic to*

be placed in there [sic] cabinet to keep alive the memory of what that tree had witnessed, of which this Box is made from a piece of the root.

As recently as March 2006, Dorrance Wright presented a piece of the Treaty Elm to the library in Levittown, Pennsylvania. A one-time foreman at Kensington's Neafie and Levy Shipyard was in the neighborhood at the time the tree blew down in March 1810. He was one of the men who helped to cut it up, and the wood was distributed among them as relics. After he died, his stepson Robert D. Webb, employed as a carpenter at the PRR Kensington freight station in Philadelphia, obtained possession of his father's cut of the Great Elm. Several ornaments were made of the wood, and there were several pieces remaining, one of which was given to the library.

In 2007, a Treaty Tree box emerged in Northeast Philadelphia. It was a small box with an inlaid liberty shield on the top cover. The inscription on the inside of the box read:

The Liberty Shield in the top is from the Elm Treaty Tree Kensington. H. Manderson, June 8th 1865.

A box with an inscription under the lid reading: "The Liberty Shield in the top is from the Elm Treaty Tree Kensington. H. Manderson, June 8th 1865." *Courtesy John Connors Collection.*

Small, round box made from the Treaty Elm, circa 1810–36. Given to the father of T. Powel by Roberts Vaux. *Courtesy John Connors Collection.*

Research on the box showed that it was probably constructed by Henry Manderson, a member of an old Kensington lumber family. The owner of the box did not know its history; it was a gift to him from forty years ago. After an introduction between John Connors (director of the Penn Treaty Museum) and the owner of the box, the box was purchased by Connors for his museum. Connors also purchased a small circular box (with a lid) on eBay that had a manuscript note inside stating that it was given to a Mr. Powell by Roberts Vaux. Connors himself also possesses a large slice of one of the Treaty Elm's descendants.

Before the loss of the Treaty Elm, there was no need to create or erect a memorial to Penn's Treaty since the tree itself was the memorial. However, without the famed elm tree, the honored spot was in danger of disappearing forever. The riverfront of Kensington was booming, and land was in demand. A story reported in Philadelphia's *Aurora and Franklin Gazette* on April 12, 1825, gives an idea of the activity:

> *The District of Kensington at present exhibits a scene of animation in business seldom before witnessed. The hum of industry along its wharves and the building materials scattered profusely over all its streets, betoken a state of prosperous increase in wealth. Nearly 4,000 tons of shipping is on the stocks and it is intended shortly to commence two more large vessels. The street near the site of the "Treaty Tree" is to be straightened and an old building to be removed. The whole district in appearance and wealth is advancing rapidly.*

Of course, the Treaty Tree was no longer, but the spot where it once stood was becoming crowded with industry. The "old building" mentioned "to be removed" appears to have already been forgotten—it was the historic Fairman's Mansion, the place where William Penn stayed upon his arrival in Philadelphia and the building around which Anthony Palmer founded his town of Kensington.

THE FOUNDING OF THE PENN SOCIETY

Even though it was not until 1892 that the City of Philadelphia finally purchased the property to create Penn Treaty Park, it was actually much earlier when the first efforts began to save the history of that memorable place.

Roberts Vaux (1786–1836) was the first in a long line of Philadelphians who came forward after the Treaty Tree was lost to begin the dialogue that would eventually lead to erecting a memorial to honor Penn's Treaty with the Indians at Shackamaxon.

Roberts Vaux was a birthright Quaker from a prominent family who was sympathetic to the Indian cause during their time of difficult resettlement. His background of Quakerism and interest in the survival of the American Indians most likely led him to his interest in William Penn's Treaty with the Indians. Vaux was very much an activist, being a vocal abolitionist, as well as taking a great interest in the penal reforms at Eastern State Penitentiary and in the emerging public school system of Philadelphia.

John Fanning Watson (1779–1860), an antiquarian and historian, well known in Philadelphia at that time for his collection of historical artifacts

Pierre S. du Ponceau (1760–1844), Watson and Vaux were the main advocates for erecting a monument to honor Penn's Treaty with the Indians. *Courtesy of the author.*

and manuscripts, as well as for his vast knowledge of Philadelphia's history, was also an early pioneer for the recognition of Penn's Treaty. Watson and Vaux were on the same committee of history, moral science and literature at the American Philosophical Society. In an attempt to capitalize on the enthusiasm for General Lafayette's memorable visit to Philadelphia in 1824, Vaux and Watson organized the Society for the Commemoration of the Landing of William Penn, otherwise known as the Penn Society.

Lafayette's well-received visit to Philadelphia reminded people of the time, almost fifty years previous, of the years of the American Revolution. The historical interest generated by Lafayette's visit was an important period

JOHN FANNING WATSON.

John Fanning Watson (1779–1860), the Philadelphia annalist and antiquarian, was a pioneer for the recognition of Penn's Treaty; with Vaux he organized the Penn Society. *Courtesy of the author.*

Richard Peters (1743–1828), judge for the U.S. District Court of Pennsylvania, passed down Lay's oral history of the Treaty Tree to the Penn Society. *Courtesy of the author.*

Benjamin Lay (1681–1759), Quaker abolitionist, immigrated to Philadelphia in 1732. He once pointed out the Treaty Tree to Richard Peters and related its history. *Courtesy of the author.*

of time in the awakening of Philadelphians to their historic past, and with the founding of the Penn Society, it became an event that saved the memory of Penn's Treaty.

Membership to the Penn Society was open to "any person of good moral character" who was approved by the board. Early members and founders of the Penn Society—such as Roberts Vaux, John F. Watson, Pierre S. du

Ponceau, J. Francis Fisher, J. Parker Norris and others—also show up as the founders of the Historical Society of Pennsylvania, which was formed at this time as well.

The purpose of the Penn Society was "to portray the character, and perpetuate just and grateful recollections of the services of the illustrious lawgiver [William Penn] and his companions." One way they hoped to carry out this purpose was by an annual delivery of lectures and "by preserving representations of scenes of great interest; and also by constructing monuments at various points, distinguished by events that shed luster over our early annals."

The Penn Society's first meeting, on November 4, 1824, featured a sumptuous banquet held at Letitia Court, a house that was once the home of William Penn himself. The first meeting's agenda was to commemorate "Penn's landing on the American shore" in 1682 and to honor "the memory of his virtue." The Penn Society dinner turned into an annual event, and in 1825, the dinner was blessed by the presence of President John Quincy Adams.

PENN SOCIETY SUPPORTS A TREATY TREE MEMORIAL

One of the objectives of the Penn Society was to use the membership dues to erect monuments to the "fame and memory of their great founder." Roberts Vaux, in a paper titled "A Memoir on the Locality of the Great Treaty Between William Penn and the Indian Natives, in 1682" and read before the Historical Society of Pennsylvania on September 19, 1825, called on the historical society "that measures be put in train for erecting a plain and substantial Obelisk of Granite, near where the tree formerly stood at Kensington, with appropriate inscriptions."

As one newspaper reported years later on the founding of the Penn Society and the erection of the memorial:

> *Away back in 1824 some of our grave and revered citizens, who were beginning to cultivate historic tastes, assembled in a spirit of reverence for the past, ate their dinners and made their speeches and became enthusiastic over the sacred memories that hovered around their place of meeting, Penn's old cottage in Letitia Court. Here they created the Penn Society, and seventeen years after the Treaty Elm was blown down in 1810 they erected in order to preserve knowledge of where the great elm stood, for future generations,*

> *the little monument on or about the same spot. This monument, it is said, was the first erected in Philadelphia, and for this reason, if nothing else, it is fortunate that it has been preserved. There are those who claim that it commemorates only a tradition, but nevertheless, poets, patriots, philosophers and historians have accepted the story of Penn's Treaty of friendship and peace with the Indians under the great elm at Kensington.*

Thus the Penn Society erected its memorial to Penn's Treaty, an obelisk standing slightly over five feet tall and inscribed on all four faces. In a more contemporary description of the event, the *Pennsylvania Gazette* of November 24, 1827, reported the following:

> *Penn's Treaty was held at Shackamaxon, (now Kensington) as Mr. Roberts Vaux has satisfactorily shown in his memoir in the Historical transactions. That situation was selected, because it was a favorite resort of the natives, where some of the first emigrants, members of the Society of Friends, originally bound for West New Jersey, had taken up their bode, more than a year antecedently to the arrival of Penn in the Delaware.*
>
> *The Elm Tree, the stately and ancient land mark, so long an object of respect, was prostrated during a storm in 1810, and soon after that event, many other changes occurred in that vicinity, contributing to obliterate the remembrance of the place where, and perhaps also, in some measure, to obscure the principles upon which that Treaty was made. To rescue the locality from oblivion, and to preserve in honorable recollection, the righteous deeds performed upon it, so far as these ends might be within their power, was a duty, which the Directors of the Penn Society were anxious to fulfill. A Committee was accordingly appointed, consisting of Roberts Vaux, Joseph Parker Norris, and John Bacon, Esquires, with authority to cause a suitable memorial to be placed there, if the proprietor of the soil would grant permission. The consent of the heirs of the late Mr. Matthew Vandusen being obtained, a marble monument has been erected on the spot...The position of this monument is on the bank of the Delaware, at Kensington, near the intersection of Hanover and Beach Streets.*

This obelisk was the first public monument erected in the city of Philadelphia, although at the time of its placement it was actually the District of Kensington, not the city of Philadelphia. Kensington did not become a part of the city until Philadelphia County was consolidated into the city in 1854.

PENN SOCIETY REPORTED ON NATIONWIDE

The formation of the Penn Society created quite a stir and was of national interest, as this sort of society was one of the first of its kind. It consisted of many of Philadelphia's elites, and its annual dinner attracted many notable people. Newspapers from as far away as Florida, Georgia, Louisiana, Indiana and Washington, D.C., reported on the activities of the Penn Society, and as a result the nation became more aware of Penn's Treaty with the Indians.

The New Hampshire Statesman and Concord Register reported on the Penn Society activities on November 5, 1825, after President Adams attended the annual dinner of the society. A New Orleans newspaper, the *Louisiana Advertiser*, on November 27, 1826, reported on the Penn Society meeting, the address by Thomas J. Wharton and the dinner afterward at the Masonic Hall. The *Raleigh Register* and *North-Carolina Gazette* published reports of this same meeting earlier, on November 10.

Several Washington, D.C. newspapers were found reporting on the Penn Society, as witnessed by stories in the *Daily National Journal* of October 30, 1826, and October 29, 1827, as well as when the *Daily National Intelligencer* noted on November 29, 1826, that "the Directors of the Penn Society of Philadelphia have appointed a Committee to inquire into the practicability of placing a Memorial to designate the spot upon which the Elm Tree stood at Kensington."

The Indianapolis newspaper, the *Indian Journal*, reported on November 27, 1828, about the Penn Society's annual meeting for that year (the annual meeting is held on the anniversary of the landing of William Penn, October, 24, 1682). In the news story, the paper showed the historical respect and humanitarian nature of the Penn Society, as it listed the various toasts in the order that were made at the dinner:

1. *The Anniversary of the Landing of William Penn*
2. *William Penn*
3. *The Pilgrim Fathers of Pennsylvania*
4. *The Treaty under the Elm—"a text book for diplomats, whether monarchical or republican."*
5. *Old Upland, the seat of the first Pennsylvania government*

6. The Great Law
7. The First Tariff, which taxes the importation of Negro Slaves, Rum, and other Spirits
8. The Fragments of the Lenni Lenape, once the powerful sovereigns of Pennsylvania, may no cruel or avaricious hand disturb them in their last retreat.
9. Universal Education
10. The Three Lower Counties
11. Auld Lang Syne—the day of Old Philadelphia
12. Pennsylvania from the Delaware to Lake Erie
13. The Memory of the late venerable Judge Peters

There was also a toast volunteered by a guest:

> *Our ancient and faithful allies the Delaware Indians, wherever they may be carried by the destiny of nations, in Illinois, or Arkansas, we ask humanity to themselves and justice to their history.*

Notable in the newspaper account, the Penn Society made two toasts to the American Indians, as well as a toast to Penn's Treaty with the Indians, all delivered with "respect and honor to the two parties and their treaty."

CHAPTER 3

THE FIRST DECLINE, FERNON'S ATTEMPTS AND THE FOUNDING OF THE PARK

When the Penn Treaty Memorial was erected, it was looked upon as a "temporary affair"—the Penn Society proposed to establish a much larger monument at a later date, but this never came to pass and the original monument stayed in its place.

At the end of the two decades (1827–47) following the original erection of the Penn Treaty Memorial, the obelisk began to show signs of neglect. After only twenty years, there were signs of a decline in the upkeep and care of the monument, as many of the original founders of the Penn Society had died and interest had waned. Roberts Vaux, the real impetus for the erection of the monument, died in 1836, followed in 1844 by Penn Treaty researcher Pierre S. du Ponceau at the age of eighty-eight. John Fanning Watson lived until 1860; however, the Penn Treaty Memorial was more Vaux's idea, and Watson was getting on in age and lived out in Germantown, a considerable distance from the monument. The task of caring for the obelisk seems to have passed from the downtown elites who first erected the monument into the hands of the local Kensingtonians who lived near the monument.

One newspaper reporter, writing in a Philadelphia paper (*North American and Daily Advertiser*) on January 28, 1845, stated that:

> *The monument in Kensington on the site of the old elm tree, in commemoration of the celebrated Penn Treaty, ought at present to attract attention. It seems that very little regard is paid to it generally, the care for some time past*

> *taken having been bestowed by several citizens of the neighborhood, and perhaps one or two others who have felt an interest in the preservation of the memento and its appearances. We learn that at the present time the fencing around it is in a dilapidated condition, and that a part of it has been thrown down.—Something should be done by our authorities or public institutions* [to] *secure the ground upon which the monument is erected, and to preserve the whole from injury.*

The very next year, workmen employed to excavate the site of the treaty grounds in Kensington dug up a large number of roots of the old elm tree. This circumstance caused "much of a stir among the denizens of the District and others, all of whom were anxious to carry off some portion of the precious relic, to keep as a remembrance of a scene celebrated in the history of the founding and settlement of Pennsylvania." This might have been the occasion when one "Miss Eyre" came into the possession of some of the roots of the Treaty Elm. There is an account in which Miss Eyre dug up the Treaty Tree roots and took them with her when she moved from Kensington to Bethlehem, Pennsylvania. She lived in a quaint old house, known as the "First Moravian Store," now torn down. The old roots stood in her parlor and were used as a "whatnot," and their curious appearance attracted the attention of visitors. They were deposited by her executrix and niece, Miss Rosalie Tiers, in the museum of the "Young Men's Moravian Missionary Society," at Bethlehem, Pennsylvania.

One problem that arose and was noted in the *Journal of the Philadelphia County Board of 1848*, is that "the Penn Society did not, neither as buyer nor renter, secure a right to the occupancy of one foot of the soil covered by the 'monument,' hence the monument remains where it is upon mere sufferance and may be moved and the space cleared whenever the order to do so shall be given." Apparently, at the time the Penn Society erected its monument it had an understanding with the Vandusen family, but later generations of the family did not appear to have taken an interest in the preservation of the memorial, particularly since the land had become far more valuable.

In this 1848 report, the county board recommended "in strong language" the acquisition of this property, stating, "The failure to act would cause unceasing regret for an irreparable loss." The fact that members of the county board argued so strongly in 1848 to purchase the property on which the Penn Treaty Monument was erected, in order to save it from oblivion, is rather startling when one thinks that the land surrounding the Penn Treaty Monument was not actually purchased for the founding of a park until over forty years later. To get a better understanding of this first attempt to create Penn Treaty Park, we take a look at the man behind it, Thomas S. Fernon.

THOMAS S. FERNON'S ATTEMPT TO CREATE PENN TREATY PARK

In 1852, the Philadelphia County Board published a "Report of the Committee on Roads and Bridges, of the County Board, on the Subject of the Proposed Purchase of Penn's Treaty Ground, for Public Use." This report gives an account of the actions at that time of an attempt by Thomas S. Fernon to get the Philadelphia County Board to purchase the treaty ground. At this time (1852), Philadelphia County and the city of Philadelphia were two separate entities. It was not until 1854 that Philadelphia County was consolidated into the city of Philadelphia.

Fernon was born on April 24, 1818, in Kensington and died June 10, 1896, at his home at 1402 Spruce Street in Philadelphia. He spent most of his youth in Kensington. In 1841, he started to study with the portrait painter John P. Merrill and for a time continued this new profession. In the autumn of 1843, Fernon was elected on the Democratic ticket as a member of the House of Representatives of Pennsylvania. He was elected again in 1846 and reelected in 1847. In 1852, a large majority elected him as a Democrat to the Pennsylvania State Senate over the Native American and Whig candidates. At this time, he organized, raised the money for and built the North Pennsylvania Railroad and was the first president of that railroad. Subsequently, he was also the president of the Chester Valley Railroad. In 1857, he started the publication of the *United States Mining and Railroad Register*, which in 1860 was sold to the Pennsylvania Railroad Company. At the outbreak of the Civil War, he left the Democratic Party and retired from politics. When he died in 1896, he left a widow and a son.

In 1852, Fernon appears to have sat on the Philadelphia County Board with a position on the committee on roads and bridges. In that year, an act by the Pennsylvania State Assembly was passed to open Beach Street at the Penn Treaty Grounds, and Fernon's committee was inquiring about what had taken place up to the present time concerning this act. A recounting of the actions leading up to 1852 was written up. At a county board meeting on September 18, 1848, the committee of estimates was requested to report to the board "the conditions upon which the county can purchase, for public use, the lot of ground known as the site of Penn's Treaty, held with the Indian nations, in the year 1682." The request was read a second time, considered and finally agreed to. This was the primary movement of a series of events that involved Fernon and his attempt to create a park to honor Penn's Treaty. This action was followed up by several reports and other actions.

Another meeting of the county board was held on December 26, 1848. Fernon was also on the committee of estimates, which gave a report at this meeting on the Penn Monument:

> *The present condition of the treaty ground is amply suggestive of regretful comment. The monument, which is a plain marble shaft, upon a double square base, measuring from the foundation to the summit, five feet nine inches, does not, as the inscription upon it asserts, mark the site of the Great Elm Tree. The actual site of the Treaty Tree, which was blown down on the third day of March, 1810* [actually March 5], *is marked by a post, put into the ground at the time of the disaster, and which still occupies its original position, at the distance of about fifty-one feet in a line south, southeast from the monument erected by the Penn Society, in the year 1827, and placed where it is now to be seen, by permission of the owners of the ground. The Penn Society did not, either as buyer or renter, secure a right to the occupancy of one foot of the soil covered by the "monument," and embraced within the dilapidated paling which once surrounded it; hence, the "monument" remains where it is, upon mere sufferance, and may be moved, and the space cleared, whenever the order to do so shall be given.*
>
> *The Treaty lot being private property, of course it may at any time be built upon, or disposed of in such a manner as may forever bury it from view, and bar the public from its possession. If this misfortune were to happen, it can readily be imagined how sincere would be the sorrow, and universal the regret, for its irreparable loss; and it may happen, if measures be not now adopted to avert it, inasmuch as the later proprietor divided the estate into several portions, among his heirs, either of whom may at any time dispose of a separate interest.*

Fernon's committee then went on to suggest that the county board needed to take action to guard the treaty grounds by purchasing the property. A new resolution was adopted by the board, with an appropriation of money made and a request authorized for the county commissioners to make the purchase of the Penn Treaty Grounds. However, problems soon set in for the county commissioners and excuses started to be made to thwart the purchase. One such excuse was that the county had no right to purchase and hold real estate except in cases provided for by special act. Others suggested that the county board had no power to confer any such authority.

A Boston newspaper (the *Boston Daily Atlas*) picked up on the story of trying to save the Penn Treaty Monument site. On January 1, 1849, while discussing the hoped-for $4,500 appropriation by the Philadelphia County Commissioners, the reporter mentioned that

> *the* [Penn Treaty] *ground is now covered by huge piles of boards from an adjacent saw mill, but for this timely appropriation it would inevitably have been built over. Within a few years back this portion of the suburb of Kensington has become crowded with factories, mills, and ship-yards, and even the Monument has not more than a dozen square feet of ground appropriated to it.*

The state legislature was appealed to and an act passed, dated April 9, 1849, which stated "that the County Commissioners of Philadelphia County are hereby vested with power and authority to purchase and hold, for public use, the lot or piece of ground known as the site of Penn's Treaty with the Indians." The county commissioners, nevertheless, "still declined to prosecute the negotiation to an issue, the fiscal year, meanwhile, expired, and the sum appropriated by the County Board, as an initiatory item, reverted to the County Treasury, and was absorbed in the expenditures of the succeeding fiscal year." Thus another attempt to purchase the Penn Treaty Grounds had failed.

The next attempt by Fernon came when the Pennsylvania state legislature approved an act to widen Beach Street on April 26, 1852. The act read as follows:

> *From its present southernmost line, one hundred and fifty feet, beginning on the line of Hanover street, and thence extending eastwardly parallel with the line of said Beach street, at least one hundred and fifty feet, so that the area to be dedicated to public use, shall be two hundred feet eastwardly from the western line of Hanover street; said street to be opened as soon as practicable to the width herein prescribed, as streets and roads are opened, under existing laws in the city and county of Philadelphia; the Commissioners of the District of Kensington shall have power to enclose a plot in the center of said area, not exceeding one hundred feet square, and shall place, or authorize to be placed therein, a monument or other memorial, to commemorate an event identified with the settlement and history of the Commonwealth.*

The way the law was written allowed Beach Street to be widened to a width much larger than needed but then also allowed the District of Kensington to set aside a one-hundred-foot by one-hundred-foot park in the center of Beach Street just north of Hanover (Columbia) Street with fifty-foot-wide streets on all four sides of the square. The square could then be used to place the Penn Treaty Monument. The monument would be moved to this site, the original site of the Treaty Tree, and a fence would be placed around the square—thus the monument would be saved from obscurity, and the site of Penn's Treaty would be kept sacred.

Fernon's report stated that if there was any complaint "to the comparative narrowness of the stipulated boundaries of the proposed purchase," the complaint ("to have force or reason") should be "lodged against the neglect or omission of those who lived at an earlier day, to buy the ground when improvements were sparse in the neighborhood, and while yet the primitive elm, sycamore, and beach studded some of the adjacent lots, and waved their foliage over the green bluff and pebbly shore." The author of the report goes on to state:

> *Then—and the period is scarce beyond a score of years gone—a beautiful park, of grassy, undulating surface, planted with native forest trees, and stretching from Hanover street to Palmer, and from Beach street to the river, might have been purchased and dedicated to public use; but that time is past, and with it departed the opportunity to obtain ground for any purpose, by acre measure, in that locality.*

Fernon was correct. The time had passed to be able to purchase land cheaply on the riverfront, and it would take another forty years for the actual realization of Penn Treaty Park to come to fruition and then another eighty-seven years for the park to be able to expand to its current size.

Fernon goes on in his report to chastise the procrastinators of the neighborhood. He wrote:

> *It is...a waste of words, as well in view of the condition of the County Treasury...to discuss now the propriety or purchasing a broader Beach street front at the Treaty place than is prescribed in the act of the Assembly... The promptings of common sense, and the obvious dictates of prudence and good policy, alike demonstrate the necessity of first obtaining the Treaty site, before indulging idle plans of impracticable magnitude. If too much be sought, nothing will be attained but the mortifying consequences of an*

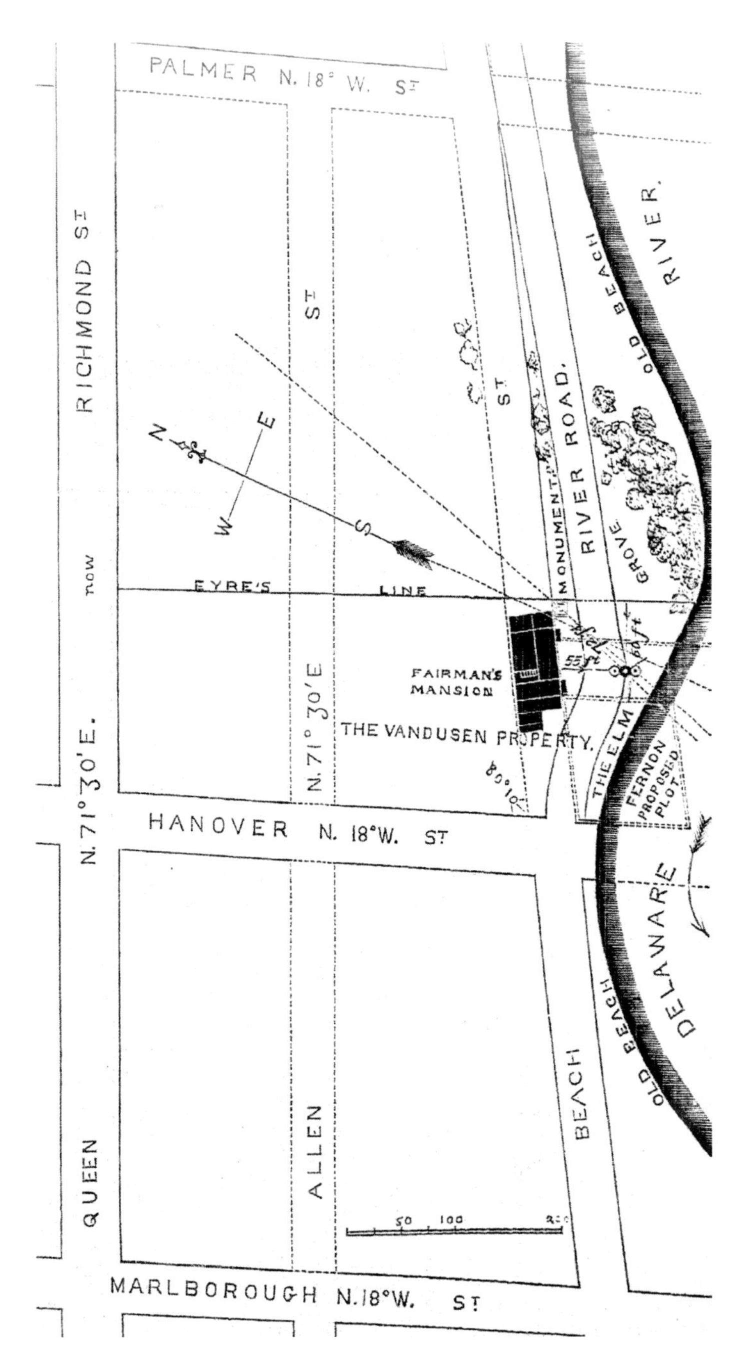

A map showing the exact location of Fairman's Mansion, the Treaty Elm and the original Delaware River shoreline, taken from *Sloan's Architectural Journal & Builder's Review*, 1868. *Courtesy of the author.*

unwise act, and the sting of reproaches, flung from the lips of an indignant community. What is demanded by manifest public sentiment in the city and county, is, that no needless procrastination be permitted by the tribunals and officers having authority in the premises, but that the law be enforced, the ground secured, and such equivalent in money given for it, as will justly reimburse its owners.

Fernon appears to have been dumbfounded that there was any hesitation to purchase the Penn Treaty Grounds and make the area a public park. Why the community, the county board and the commissioners of the District of Kensington, or even those that actually owned the Treaty Tree ground, would forestall something of such importance as saving the sacred place of Penn's Treaty was astonishing. As Fernon wrote:

What need of hesitation, what excuse for delay? If issue as to price, in fixing the award arise, there need be no lack of disinterested and impartial testimony to rule the decision, and give it solid, binding force. The ground to be taken for the enclosure and avenue, is worth the same in dollars as other ground in the vicinity, and comprising equal space and eligibility of location. As a resting-place for the foundation-stone of any sort of edifice devoted to domestic ends or the mechanic arts, it has no intrinsic money value, which is not possessed by other property near it, and quite as available for buildings in all respects. Lots fitted for objects of enterprise and pursuits of gain, may be had in any number inside the municipal bounds, while but one spot on the earth's surface marks the site of the Treaty Elm. There is, therefore, every incentive for its preservation, and every reason for its transfer to public ownership and care. If made a location for the walls of a dwelling, storehouse, or workshop, the touching interest that pervades the mist of its historical associations, would be merged in the indignation elicited by the sight of its desecration.

Following up on the Pennsylvania state legislature's bill to allow the widening of Beach Street, there was also passed an act on May 4, 1852, to allow the "District of Kensington and County of Philadelphia, to extend the southern boundary line of the enclosure on the site of Penn's Treaty southward, to the line of Delaware Avenue." What this did was allow the District of Kensington to expand the boundaries of the park, making it 50 percent larger (150 by 150 feet as opposed to 100 by 100 feet). It must be remembered that, at this point in time, Delaware Avenue was not yet laid out, but a proposal was afloat for it to be opened in order to help the growing commerce on the Delaware River. Originally, Delaware Avenue was to be opened east of Beach Street.

Thus the park that Fernon envisioned was to be bounded on the east by Delaware Avenue, west by Beach Street, south by Hanover (Columbia) Street and north by an as-yet-unnamed street. The order of events that needed to happen to create the park was that Beach Street had to be expanded; the District of Kensington had to acquire the one hundred square feet of land; and when Delaware Avenue was resurveyed and opened, the park had to be expanded by 50 percent. The county was to become owner of the space fronting the park on the river, and a proposal of creating a "Treaty Pier" was mentioned as a possibility.

All did not go as planned for Fernon. The District of Kensington commissioners suspended the proceedings on resurveying Delaware Avenue, and that project was sent to die in a committee. A jury was created to assess the damages to the property owners who would lose their land in the creation of the park. Arguments ensued over the amount of monies the properties were evaluated at, with Jehu Eyre stating that $500 was not enough and that his damages were over $1,000. The District of Kensington wanted the state legislature to pay half the damages ($25,500). Counsel did not represent the county board during the proceedings in the assembly for the widening of Beach Street, and the District of Kensington declined to now send counsel to the assembly for further proceedings. When the day came for the hearing on the matter of the widening of Beach Street and the Penn Treaty Grounds, it was set aside by the court.

The Historical Society of Pennsylvania had previously approved the action of the legislature and expressed a hope that the commissioners of Kensington might be induced to take early action, but the entire matter came to a halt and would not be revived again until the City of Philadelphia purchased the property in 1892.

H.G. Jones Jr., the historical society's Elm Tree Treaty committee member, stated:

> *So far as the expression of public opinion has been enlisted the indications are strongly in favor for the purchase of this ground. The record of Penn's treaty or conference is a singular feature in the early history of Pennsylvania, unparalleled in the annals of any other Commonwealth, and the spot where the simple touching drama was performed by the Quaker and the Indians should long ago have been made one of the chief attractions of Philadelphia.*

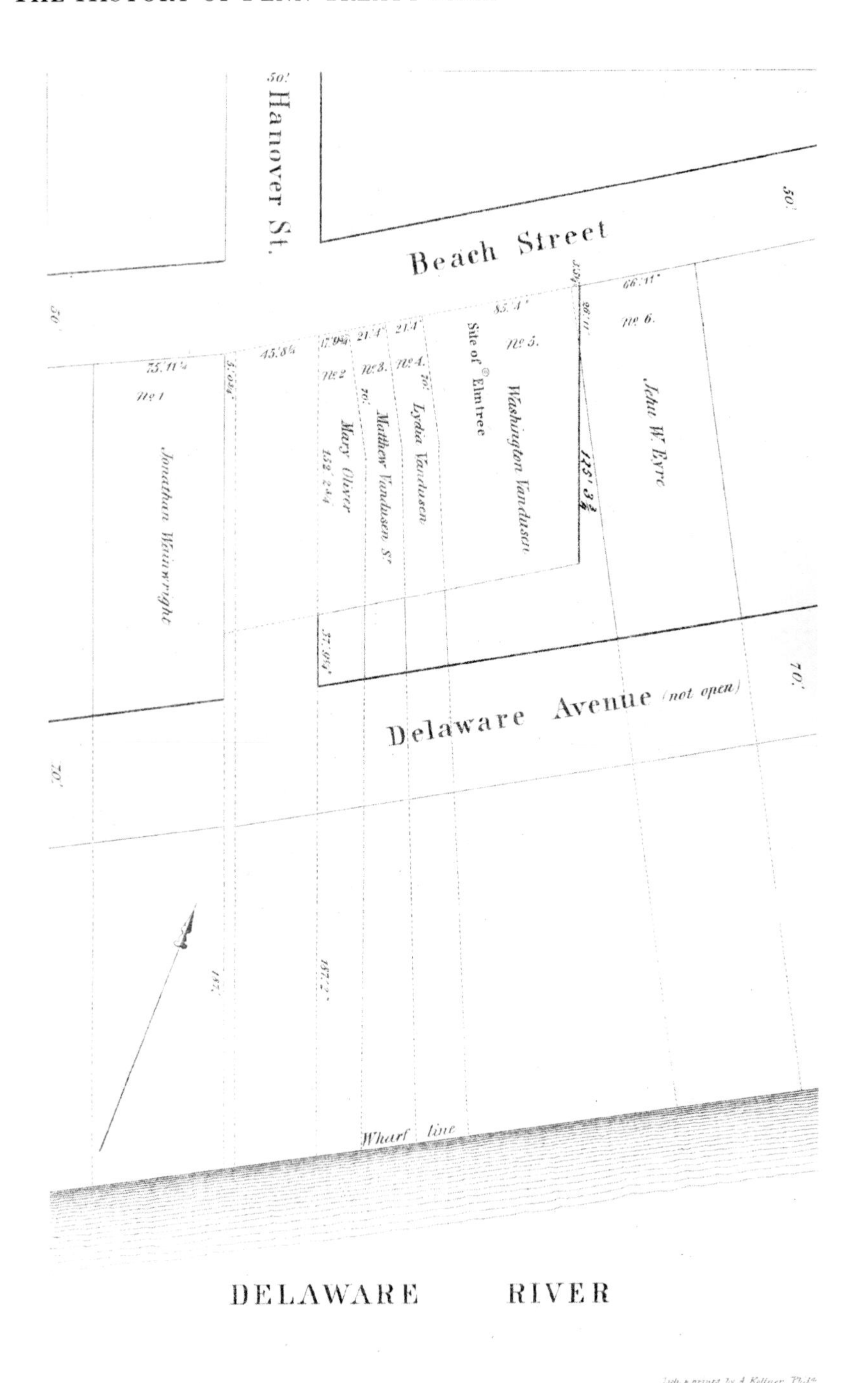

A map showing the properties that were to be affected by Thomas S. Fernon's Penn Treaty Park in 1852. The plan was not carried out. *Courtesy of the author.*

> *The spectator, whether a tourist from abroad or a citizen belonging in our midst, is in either case shocked and mortified at the spectacle presented in its dilapidated condition, and turns away mourning the indifference which permits it so to remain.*

Fernon, probably from disgust and realizing that his dream for the creation of Penn Treaty Park was breaking apart, discharged his committee from further discussion of the subject. An opportunity was missed to create Penn Treaty Park, and the Penn Treaty Monument would have to wait another forty years before it found a permanent home.

Between Thomas S. Fernon's attempt to create Penn Treaty Park and the actual creation of the park in 1893, the paper record shows very little interest in the Penn Treaty Monument. There were several attempts to have money allocated to provide funds to care for the monument and the iron fence that surrounded it, but no serious attempt appears to have been made to create a park.

THREATS OF THE SALE OF THE TREATY MONUMENT

By 1856, the "For Rent" signs started to appear at the Penn Treaty site. Washington Vandusen, the son of Matthew Vandusen and owner at this time, put an advertisement in Philadelphia's *North American and United States Gazette:*

> *Penn Treaty Wharf to Let—The whole part of the above Wharf to be let. River front of 180 feet. Apply to W. Vandusen, Hanover, 2d door above Beach St., Kensington.*

The advertisement ran for several days, adding that the depth of the lot was 333 feet.

In the summer of 1868, the architect Samuel Sloan founded a publication titled *Sloan's Architectural Review & Builders' Journal.* The first issue came out in July 1868 and contained an article by Charles J. Lukens titled "The Penn Treaty-Ground and a Monument to William Penn." Besides giving a long background history of Penn's Treaty with the Indians, Lukens's article goes on to critique Thomas S. Fernon's attempt to create a Penn Treaty Park. According to Lukens, Fernon's planned Penn Treaty Square did not even include the actual site of the Treaty Elm within its borders and had actually left it outside of the park, underneath one of the proposed streets that were to surround the square.

Other than leaving the site of the Treaty Tree outside of the park, Lukens agreed with Fernon's plans; however, it was not as easy to convince the politicians, as the actual cost for purchasing the land needed for the proposed size of the park was now at $600,000 for the land and about $300,000 for the buildings on the land. Coupled with the cost of building a pier, landscaping, moving the monument and other projects that would need to be done, the cost of the park was now estimated at over $2,000,000.

On February 20, 1868, Alexander Adaire, a local Kensington lumberman who served in the Pennsylvania Statehouse, introduced a joint resolution in the House to appropriate $5,000 to repair the Penn Treaty Monument. The resolution was not acted upon until the following month when, on March 27, it was reported that the issue of "repairing the Penn Treaty Monument in the 18th Ward came up," and a Mr. Hickman moved to amend the resolution by reducing the appropriation to $2,500, providing the citizens of Philadelphia subscribe a like amount. Forty-seven legislators agreed and thirty dissented, and the measure passed. Locally, Philadelphia legislators Adaire, Dally, Holgate, Hong, Kleckner, McGinnis, Mullen, Michael, Stokes, Thorn, Whetham and Speaker Davis voted yes, with Mr. Bull voting no. It is unclear if the citizens of Philadelphia ever raised the needed $2,500 in matching funds.

In September 1870, yet another resolution was introduced, this time in the common councils of Philadelphia. A Mr. Logan offered a resolution to appoint a joint committee of three people from each chamber (common and select councils) to purchase the Penn Treaty Grounds. The resolution was referred to committee. The finance committee reported on the resolution, and it was promptly postponed.

In April 1872, Washington Vandusen again began to place advertisements in the local papers about the Penn Treaty Wharf; however, this time he was offering for sale equipment from his lumber and sawmill business:

> *For Sale, to be Removed. Penn Treaty Marine Railway. Cylinder Boiler, 30 feet by 30 inches; Circular Saws, Jig Saws, Belting, &c. W. Vandusen, Penn Treaty Wharf, 1309 Beach Street, Kensington.*

This advertisement ran during the month of April 1872, as well as in September 1872. His September advertisement showed him to be selling the Marine Railway and renting the wharf:

Penn Treaty Wharf to Let and a Marine Railway for sale, with steam or horse power, jig and circular saws and fixtures. Apply to W. Vandusen, 324 Madison ave., Phila.

By November 20, 1872, Vandusen no longer advertised the Marine Railway but was looking to rent or sell the Penn Treaty Wharf. Presumably Vandusen, who was about sixty-seven years old in 1872, was retiring, selling the business and looking to dispose of the property, as well.

More time went by. In a city council session on December 16, 1880, local councilman Benjamin M. Faunce, of the Eighteenth Ward, introduced a resolution instructing the commissioner of markets and city property to "employ a portion of the coping and railing" that they were removing from around Washington Square "to fence in the Penn Treaty Monument." Faunce's resolution was referred to the finance committee.

Faunce came from an eighteenth-century Kensington family who put the "F" in Fishtown. Members of the Faunce family made up the largest family of fishermen on the Delaware River and played an important role in the development of the area. Faunce was probably concerned about protecting the Penn Treaty Memorial because for years the great majority of people forgot about the existence of this monument. It was "friendless and alone, frequently buried beneath piles of lumber, its face hidden from the sun and the eyes of man." Many times there were threats to remove it by the owners of the property on which it stood, but for some reason or other it remained.

An indication at this time that the Penn Treaty Wharf might have become a hazard is recorded on July 1, 1886, when it was reported that John Dietz, a sixty-five-year-old man of 1225 Leopard Street, had his leg fractured when one of the lumber piles that surrounded the Penn Treaty Monument fell on him. He was taken to the Episcopal Hospital.

However, the real sign of trouble at the famed Penn Treaty site happened on March 4, 1890, when there appeared a "For Sale" notice in the *Philadelphia Inquirer*. This advertisement may have been the catalyst that began the final rallying cry of Philadelphia's citizenry for the founding of Penn Treaty Park, a cry that had been voiced for eighty years, from the time the famous Elm Tree had fallen:

For Sale. Penn Treaty Wharf. This very valuable wharf and historic piece of ground is situated on the S.E. side of Beach St., beginning 60 ft. 5¾ inches N.E. from Hanover and extending from Beach Street to the River

Delaware; 85 feet 4 inches front on Beach street and 130 feet on Warden's Outside Line. This property has an average front or width of 107 feet, the width or front on the warden's outside line being about 130 feet and the width on the warden's inside line for head of docks being about 107 feet. The distance from Beach street to the warden's outside line is about 623 feet. See plan.

There is a Two-story Brick stable on the wharf. There is also a monument, with...four inscriptions on its four sides...Sale by order of Heirs—Estate of W. Van Dusen, dec'd. For further particulars apply to John Van Dusen, Sen, 2124 N. Twentieth St., Phila...Sale on Tuesday, March 11, 1890, at 12 o'clock noon, at the Philadelphia Exchange, corner Third and Walnut Sts., By M. Thomas & Sons, auctioneers, 136 S. Fourth St.

The Penn Treaty Grounds and monument were being offered for sale by the Vandusen family, and there was no legal remedy to prevent anyone from buying the property, removing the monument and clearing and building on the site. The idea that all remnants of Penn's Treaty with the Indians could disappear from this spot forever, and the actual monument sold off, became a focal point for those Philadelphians who had long desired a memorial park for Penn's Treaty at this location.

THE FOUNDING OF PENN TREATY PARK

At this same time, there was talk in Philadelphia's city council about what to do with Kensington's old West Street Burial Ground at Vienna (Berks) and Belgrade Streets. It had become dilapidated and a community eyesore. A number of families of the deceased had already removed a large number of bodies from the old cemetery and had not refilled the grave sites. The slightly elevated cemetery smelled and featured a liquid oozing out and running across the pavements. The focus of city council talks began to be centered on removing the bodies and turning this old cemetery into a public park for the residents of the area.

However, on December 16, 1891, Kensington lawyer Joseph L. Tull appeared before the city council's law committee and argued against the taking of the plot of ground at Vienna and Belgrade Streets for a public park. Tull wanted any new square to be located at the site of the Penn Treaty Monument.

Joseph L. Tull's family had been in Philadelphia since the time of William Penn, having moved to Kensington in the early nineteenth century from the Northern Liberties area. His father, John P. Tull, had a pattern-making business at Beach and Shackamaxon Streets and was partners with the Landells, the family that ran the Kensington National Bank. The Tulls first lived on Allen Street, near Shackamaxon; as they prospered, they bought one of the larger homes on Shackamaxon. Their pattern-making business was on the site of the old sugarhouse, where SugarHouse Casino now proposes a slot parlor. John P. Tull's mother was a member of the old Germantown Pastorius family.

Besides Tull, there were others in the neighborhood who started calling for a park to honor Penn's Treaty. One of the biggest advocates was the Bramble Club, led by its president, Councilman William Rowen. The Bramble Club was a social organization made up mainly of businessmen from the Eighteenth Ward (Fishtown) of Kensington. The club was formed November 10, 1889, to promote the business interests of the neighborhood. One of the programs it was involved in was the acting out of historical events. The purpose of its honoring these historical events was to keep the "Spirit of 76" alive, a reference to the glory days of the American Revolution, as many of the founders of the Bramble Club had ancestry that dated back to those days. The club held its annual banquet and anniversary party on the twenty-second of February, to honor George Washington's birthday.

Much of the organizing of the Fishtown and Kensington neighborhoods for the celebration of these historic events, in particular in involving the youth of the local schools and churches, would be carried out by the Bramble Club and its members. Eighteenth Ward city councilman and school board member William Rowen was the longtime president of the Bramble Club, and much of its success can be attributed to him. His family was one of the "Spirit of 76" families, having fought in the Revolutionary War.

Rowen, who was a funeral director on Girard Avenue, enjoyed further political support for the founding of a Penn Treaty Park from other local politicians who were members of the Bramble Club, such as William F. Stewart, the local state representative. Stewart was a lifelong resident of Kensington and a senior member of the Pennsylvania House of Representatives. He was employed by the *Philadelphia Public Ledger* newspaper, which helped get the Bramble Club a lot of attention from the press.

Rowen also had the support of Isaac D. Hetzell, of Richmond Street, who was a councilman from Kensington. Hetzell followed his father, Andrew Hetzell, into the bricklaying business and became a substantial contractor.

He parlayed his money and influence into a seat on the Philadelphia Select City Council. Hetzell introduced the necessary legislation in the select council to purchase the Penn Treaty Grounds. Today we have a playground named in Hetzell's honor at Columbia Avenue and Thompson Street.

With the elected councilmen and a state representative of Kensington all arguing in favor of the creation of Penn Treaty Park, the wheels of government began to turn. The following month it was reported in the *Philadelphia Inquirer* of January 25, 1892, that the Philadelphia City Council and the Fairmount Park Art Commission were preparing to join hands and work together for the establishment of a park to commemorate William Penn's Treaty with the Indians.

The notion of some sort of mutual cooperation on the formulation of a Penn Treaty Park had been mentioned previously at the most recent annual meeting of the Fairmount Park Art Association and was met at that time with approval by the group. Philadelphia artist John Sartain, who presided at the annual meeting of the art association, was a backer of the Penn Treaty Park idea—a combination of a public space and a site that would commemorate the historic event of Penn's Treaty. Sartain thought "it was a grand thing to do" and accordingly laid the idea before the art committee of the art association at their next meeting, and it met with approval.

Another supporter on the city council was Thomas Meehan of Germantown's Twenty-second Ward, who, it was reported, made it his "life's work" to establish new public squares on the city plans, "for greater beauty and for more air and recreation for the masses of working people in their very homes." Meehan was a world-renowned vegetable biologist, an original fellow of the Academy of Natural Sciences and a onetime president of that institution. He was a member of all the leading scientific organizations in his native England and his adopted America, as well as in Germany, France and Australia. He was a Republican councilman from the Twenty-second Ward for sixteen consecutive years, until his death in 1901. His involvement in politics seemed to be a way for him to implement his ideas of greening Philadelphia.

Meehan was born in London, England, on March 21, 1826. At the age of nineteen, he entered Kew Gardens, London, where he spent two years. Shortly after leaving Kew, he decided to emigrate, and reached America on March 22, 1848, where he worked one year as foreman with Robert Buist. Upon leaving Buist's Rosedale Nurseries, he entered the employ of Andrew Eastwick, who lived in and owned the celebrated Bartram Gardens.

After three years of service at Bartram Gardens, Meehan became gardener to Caleb Cope. Having decided to start in business for himself, he established his own nursery in Germantown in 1854 (as well as in Ambler, Pennsylvania). His specialty was growing native shrubs and trees. The business of Germantown was conducted upon Main Street, opposite "Carpenters," and in association with William Saunders. This business increased so much that he purchased the Hong and Hortter farms on Chew Street and relocated the nursery to that place. Other acres were added, and a branch for the growing of "stock" for wholesale orders was established at Dreshertown, Pennsylvania. His nursery became one of the largest and enjoyed the distinction of being the best known in America.

THOMAS MEEHAN

Thomas Meehan (1826–1901), Chestnut Hill councilman and open space advocate. He was instrumental in getting the city to purchase the ground for Penn Treaty Park. *Courtesy of the author.*

Meehan was a prolific writer who wrote up until the time of his death. He was a contributor to the *Horticulturist*, *Germantown Telegraph* and the proceedings of the Academy of Natural Sciences, amongst other similar publications. For a number of years, he was the horticultural editor of the *Philadelphia Press*, and for over thirty years he was scientific editor of the *New York Independent*. In 1859, with David Rodney King, he founded the *Gardeners' Monthly*, a periodical for all those interested in floriculture and the best of its kind in America. Meehan continued as the editor for *Gardeners' Monthly* for all its thirty-one years. Thomas Meehan also wrote a number of books, including *The American Handbook of Ornamental Trees*, *Wayside Flowers* and a four-volume work titled *The Flowers and Ferns of the United States*. In 1891, he founded and published *Meehan's Monthly*.

Edwin C. Jellett, who wrote a biography of Meehan, states that Meehan was said to have "loved children and many years of his life were given to the improvement of the Public School System of Pennsylvania." It was he who introduced "Nature Study" and "Kindergarten" into our public schools, and the care and elevation of African American children received his best attention. In recognition of this, a Germantown school was named in his honor. He was the organizer and constant champion of the small parks movement and, by his direct efforts, secured Bartram, Vernon and other small parks for the city.

Meehan was "delighted" with the art association's idea of a memorial park for Penn's Treaty since it fit into his own plans for promoting open spaces. As it happened, his council's committee had spent the previous day at the Penn Treaty Grounds and was unanimously in favor of opening a new plot there. Meehan's committee consisted of himself, Charles Roberts, Thomas Wagner, Nathan Lewis and George W. Kendrick.

With the support from the art association to commemorate the place with a "memorial group," the idea sprung to life and was empowered by the dual quantity of prestige from the government and the elites of Philadelphia's art community. This combination of the open space ideas of the council's Meehan and the support of the folks at the Fairmount Park Art Association was the alliance that was needed to finally get city approval and financial support for Penn Treaty Park.

On January 30, 1892, the city council's committee on new public squares, the Fairmount Park Art Association and the City Parks Association were all recorded as being unanimously in favor of the "new square covering the Penn Treaty grounds." Another coup for the park movement in the creation of Penn Treaty Park was the arrival of support from the City Parks Association. The following letter by that group is a witness to their support of the park:

Dear Sir:
It is an admirable suggestion to create a small park covering the site where the Penn Treaty with the Indians was made. Your suggestion seems to me a happy union of beauty and utility, since it aims to secure an additional space for fresh air and green trees, which will be greatly to the advantage of those who are unable to seek, beyond city limits, these necessities of our hot summers, and that it will also call attention perennially to an instance of just dealing with the Indians that is succinctly rare in our history. I do not know what practical obstacles stand in the way of carrying the plan into execution, but if any such exist I trust they may be speedily removed. I shall take pleasure in calling the attention of the City Parks Association to this project, and I have no doubt the association will gladly assist in furthering it.

January 25, 1892
Herbert Welsh

Gaining Herbert Welsh's support for the establishment of Penn Treaty Park was a positive development for the park enthusiasts. Besides being from the "Proper Philadelphia" class, Welsh was also one of the founders of the Indian Rights Association (IRA), which based its headquarters in Philadelphia. The IRA was a humanitarian group dedicated to influencing federal U.S. Indian policy and protecting the rights of the Indians of the United States while promoting a policy of assimilation. The IRA was the most influential American Indian reform group of its time. The backing of this American Indian rights group helped solidify the diversified support for the creation of the park.

Herbert Welsh, like Roberts Vaux in earlier days, had a special affinity and respect for the American Indians, which connected both men to the idea of a memorial park for William Penn and his Treaty of Amity and Friendship with the Indians.

ACQUIRING THE LAND FOR THE PARK

The Penn Treaty Grounds in 1892 did not present a significant site. The local newspapers reported the area as

a wharf property, which is the scene of dirt, old carts, stray chickens, broken-down fences, a shanty or two, a small brick building, and most conspicuous of all, a sign reading: For Rent or sale, Apply John K. Van Dusen.

The newspaper story went on to say that the little treaty monument, "five feet high or less," stands on the property in a corner nearest to Neafie and Levy shipyard. It was "erected by the Penn Society in 1827, and probably represented a bigger financial undertaking than a $200,000 park and $100,000 bronze group would be now." The reporter stated that "the little statue has been so often moved about over the plot that the site of the great elm tree has been lost, so that the center would as accurately memorialize the treaty as it is possible to do."

In order to build a park at this spot, three wharf properties would have to be bought—Vandusen's, Harry Bumm's and Henry Plotz's. Plotz's wharf was next to Bumm's and was the width of Hanover Street down to the river. The entirety of the three properties measured a little less than the usual size of a public square.

The aesthetics of the area were apparently not very pleasing to the reporter, as he went on to state that "the only disadvantages presented from the artistic point of view are the unattractiveness of the neighborhood, the Beach street railroad tracks and tumble down buildings in the neighborhood beyond." He ended his piece by saying that "the fitness of a memorial group on the scene of the event, and advantages of carrying the great lesson of history ennobled by art into the hearts and homes of toiling masses of Kensington, may prove to be overwhelming advantages." While a little repugnant in tone, his point was clear: a park commemorating the history of William Penn's Treaty with the Indians would be great for the neighborhood.

The following month, on February 25, it was reported that "bills were submitted to the Committee on Municipal Government" for Penn Treaty Park. Not only was Penn Treaty Park being founded at this time, but a number of other parks were proposed as well: Walmouth Park (Kensington and Frankford), Stephen E. Fotteral Square (11th and Cumberland), Forepaugh Park (Broad and Dauphin), Vernon Park in Germantown and another square at Third and Moyamensing.

On March 2, 1892, it was reported that the Philadelphia City Council passed an ordinance to place Penn Treaty Park on the city plan. Walmouth Park and the Stephen E. Fotteral Park were the only other parks from the above list that also were placed on the city plan at this time.

The very next day, ordinances were introduced into city council and referred to committees, to appropriate $83,000 for the purchase of a plot of ground for park purposes, bounded by Beach and Hanover (Columbia) Streets, the Gorgas Estate and the Delaware River, to be known as the "Penn Treaty Park."

Finally, on March 10, an ordinance was passed by city council and signed by Mayor Edwin Sydney Stuart, and with that ordinance Penn Treaty Park was officially placed on the city plan. Edwin Stuart would later go on to become the governor of Pennsylvania.

The dimensions of the new Penn Treaty Park were published in the *Philadelphia Inquirer* March 18, 1892. They were given as follows:

> *Beginning at the east corner of Hanover* [Columbia] *and Beach Streets, thence extending along the southeast side of Beach street northeastward one hundred and forty-five feet nine and three-quarter inches, to a point on the line of land now or late of Edward W. Gorgas, thence along the same south twenty-eight degrees ten minutes fifty-five seconds, east six hundred and seventeen feet eight and one-quarter inches, more or less, to the Port Wardens' line in the river Delaware, thence along the same southwestward two hundred and sixty-six feet six inches, more or less, to the northeast line of Hanover street produced and thence along the same northwestward six hundred and eighteen feet more or less to the southeast side of Beach street, the place of beginning to be called Penn Treaty Park.*

By the summer of 1892, the plans for Penn Treaty Park were drawn up, and a hearing for the park's development was to be held on July 19, 1892, by the board of surveyors. In the *Philadelphia Inquirer* of July 15, 1892, there was a notice published stating that the citizens of Philadelphia were able to view the plans for Penn Treaty Park at the office of city surveyor Joseph Mercer. Mercer, a city surveyor for the Sixth District, kept his real estate office and home at 1845 Frankford Avenue for a time before moving to the 1900 block of North Broad Street.

Back on April 22, 1892, the council's finance committee reported favorably on the ordinance condemning three acres of ground surrounding the Penn Treaty Monument in Kensington for the purposes of creating a park. The price paid for the properties was not to exceed $85,000.

THE BUSINESS OF BUILDING THE PARK

In January 1893, the Bureau of City Property budgeted $15,000 for improvements to Penn Treaty Park, which included "grading, sodding, paving, fencing, coping, and otherwise improving the park."

On March 2, 1893, Kensington state representative William Stewart introduced a bill in Harrisburg to appropriate $5,000 for the erection of a pedestal for the proposed Penn monument soon to be erected at the new Penn Treaty Park. However, on May 18, 1893, it was reported that the Pennsylvania State House's appropriations committee reacted negatively to appropriating any funds for the pedestal.

On April 12, the City of Philadelphia began advertising for bids for "repairing wharf and bulkhead at Penn Treaty Park, foot of Hanover Street." On May 30, the city was advertising for bids for "improving Penn Treaty Park." Any bids were to be sent to Abraham M. Beiter, director of the Department of Public Safety, Bureau of City Property. The bids would be accepted until June 5, 1893. The city received one bid that exceeded the appropriated amount for the park by $2,646.

One aspect of the park improvements involved the replanning of the Penn Society's Penn Treaty Monument and recutting the eroded inscriptions engraved on it. Local toughs had taken to using the monument as target practice for throwing rocks.

On May 7, 1893, it was reported that Chief Eisenhower, of the Bureau of City Property, had before him plans for Penn Treaty Park that would make it "a gem among the city's pleasure grounds." The entire wharf property was to be turned into a public square, and a handsome pavilion was to be erected at the end of the pier. The small building on the corner of Beach Street was to remain, and the area, in memory of the tree under which Penn made his famous treaty with the Indians, was to be planted exclusively with elms.

Chief Eisenhower was again in the news on July 4, 1893, when he gave a magnificent flag to Penn Treaty Park. While not officially dedicated and open, the park had already started to attract crowds. Those gathered on this Fourth of July to give speeches at the podium were President Miles of the select council; Councilmen Agnew MacBride, Charles Kitchenman, J.W. Roth and J.E. McLaughlin; Reverend J.P. Swindells of Kensington Methodist Episcopal " Old Brick" Church; and Henry Bumm, who had inherited the property from Matthew Vandusen, the pioneer shipbuilder in the city.

A local newspaper went on to state:

> *Amid hearty plaudits and to the tune of the "Star Spangled Banner" Charles A.B. Hetzel, the little son of Councilman Hetzel, of the Eighteenth Ward, unfurled the flag, and as it slowly floated in the breeze, there fell from it a huge shower of small flags, which were eagerly scrambled for by those in the audience...It was notable that in the large audience could be seen the faces*

of many of the old-time residents of Fishtown, and by their countenances they showed that they warmly welcomed the display of patriotism in their midst. Penn Treaty Park, when properly prepared, promises to be one of the most delightful public breathing spots in the city.

In September 1893, as the park was nearing completion and ready to be dedicated, Councilman Meehan, who had been instrumental in helping to create the park, presented to city council a lithographic copy of Benjamin West's painting of *William Penn's Treaty with the Indians*. The descendants of Penn's family had sent the lithograph to Meehan, but Meehan felt it really should belong to the city. The Penn family sent it to Meehan as a tribute for his services for helping to make Penn Treaty Park become a reality.

On October 8, 1893, excitement began to build as the park was nearly ready to be dedicated. After long years of neglect and misuse, the famous Penn Treaty Grounds, a little over two acres, were going to be honored forever with a public square for all to enjoy.

Penn Treaty Park's Opening Day Celebration—October 28, 1893

As the opening day of Penn Treaty Park approached, newspapers began reporting on the events that would mark the celebration. William Rowen and the Bramble Club took the lead role in promoting and carrying out the celebration of the opening of the park. The creation of Penn Treaty Park was one of Rowen's lifelong projects, along with having Girard Avenue extended and the Aramingo Canal closed.

A veterans group—General D.B. Birney, Camp No. 13—was expected to "turn out strong" for the opening of Penn Treaty Park on October 28, 1893. Another Philadelphia newspaper reported on other activities that were in preparation:

The Red Men are making great preparations for the 211th Anniversary of the landing of William Penn in Philadelphia, which will be observed on Saturday, October 28. Eighteen tribes will participate. Exercises will begin at 3 P.M. After the orchestra plays "America," William Rowen, president of the Bramble Club, will deliver an address, to be followed by the "Star Spangled Banner," quartet; oration by a member of the I.O.R.M.; benediction. Evening, line will form north and south on Shackamaxon street and Frankford road; move at 7:30. Chief Marshall, William Rowen; Cavalcade Marshal, Thomas Swan; committee of Bramble Club, William F. Stewart, chairman; Bramble Club, Vice-President Isaac Goodwin in command; tribes of I.O.R.M. in costume; delegations of Knights of the Golden Eagle; American Mechanics; Knights of Pythias; civic bodies.

The route will be Girard avenue to Fifth, to Norris, to Frankford road, to Girard avenue, to Otis, to Richmond, to Hanover, to Penn Treaty Park, where a grand display of fireworks will take place. The afternoon program will be carried out at Penn Treaty Park, foot of Hanover street. The committee of the Bramble Club are: Representative William F. Stewart, Councilman William Rowen, Isaac Goodwin, Adam Belzer, Charles Fortner, William R. Weoters, William Carr, Joseph Rochelle, Dallas Smith, James Coulter, Fred Shuman, R.F. Biddell, William Zehner, Charles Foster, Charles Siner, and W.H. Brady.

Finally, all the various organizations were in readiness, and on the 211th anniversary of William Penn's sailing up the Delaware River, Penn Treaty Park had its official opening with a grand celebration. Papers across the country reported on the event, with estimates of ten thousand to fifteen thousand people in attendance. The Bramble Club, headed by Kensington councilman William Rowen, performed a reenactment of the arrival of William Penn.

Newspapers reported on the tremendous crowd that clamored to see all the various events, including a huge parade the likes of which Philadelphia had not seen in years:

Every foot of ground in the Park was occupied by men, women and children. The house-tops in the vicinity were black with people, and the decks of boats in the river, the wharves, and, in fact every point of vantage were filled with spectators. The important events of October 28, 1682, were re-enacted in the presence of the great multitude.

A boat representing the good ship Welcome, speeded by wind and tide, sailed rapidly up the Delaware and anchored opposite the park. A small boat put off for the shore and, soon William Penn, wearing a broad-brimmed hat, knee breeches, and buckles and a wide blue sash, stepped upon the shore. As he landed, accompanied by sailors, and his associates, all the steam craft near by in the harbor blew their whistles. A red-coated British officer, an interpreter, and a number of residents attired in brown clothes, broad white collars, and old-time tower hats met the newcomers at the wharf and escorted them to the site of the historic elm tree.

About the wigwams near by were the old white-haired Chief Tamonend or Tammany and many members of the Delaware and Susquehanna tribes. The Indians were attired in picturesque garb, and with their blankets and warm moccasins were undoubtedly more comfortably clothed than were the scantly-attired aborigines who met the famous Quaker two hundred and eleven years ago. Over blazing fagots the treaty was conducted, the chief and his braves being seated on the ground, and receiving from the interpreter the assurances of peace and amity proposed by Penn.

After the pipe of peace was smoked, Penn and his associates returned to the Welcome, while the red men went into ecstasy over their presents.

Squads from nine Grand Army posts fired salutes with cannons and muskets, and thus ended the spectacular part of the program.

A stage for speakers had been erected on the north side of the park, and still farther to the north were raised seats accommodating many hundreds of people. A platform on the east side of the stage was filled with several hundred school children, while all about these temporary structures surged the great mass of people who stood up for two hours while the exercises were being conducted. Councilman William Rowan, president of the Bramble Club, an organization of business men formed to promote the interests of the Eighteenth Ward, presided.

It was largely through the efforts of Councilman Rowen that the ground now used for the park was purchased by the city. Mr. Rowen made a speech that was loudly cheered. He said the grand old district of Kensington took this opportunity to show to Councils and the Mayor their appreciation of the acts that gave this breathing place to the northeast section of the city. "The Bramble Club," he stated, "will unite with other organizations to erect a monument in the Park to William Penn."

Charles C. Conley, great chief of records of the Great Council of the United States Improved Order of Red Men, delivered an oration. He said the future of our country rested with the girls, and the children on the platform applauded. The boys, he said, are to be the policemen of the country, by which, he added, he meant to pay a high compliment, for a guardian of the peace, whether he be president or patrolman, occupies an honorable position. He reviewed the circumstances of the treaty and, concluding, said: "If we will ever recollect that in unity there is strength; if we follow the example of William Penn and his friend Tammany, who practiced that divine maxim while on earth of 'Glory to God in the highest, on earth peace and good will among men,' then will we ever be the chosen of God, and the happiest people on His footstool, and under our starry flag a free republic forever."

Other addresses were made by Thomas K. Donnally, great chief of records of Pennsylvania, and David Conn, great sachem of Pennsylvania of the Order of Red Men. The singing was done by schoolchildren, directed by Sarah A. Gilbert, supervising principal of the Adaire Grammar School, and James Simmington. The invocation and benediction were pronounced by Reverend William Swindells.

In the evening, Kensington was brilliantly illuminated. Stores and residences were gay with flags, buntings and lanterns. In the parade was the Bramble Club, with a float representing Penn and his attendants. The second division was made up of the Order of the Red Men. The military division followed, with Grand Army Veterans, Knights of the Golden Eagle, Junior Order of U.S. Mechanics and Nights of Pythias. Volunteer firemen, New Year clubs and citizens in carriages brought up the rear. The procession was reviewed at Richmond and Hanover Streets.

The parade was more attractive than any that had been given in the city for some time. The floats of the Order of the Red Men were magnificent, especially those presented by Narragansett Tribe, No. 43, representing scenes in the life of Captain John Smith that culminated in his marriage to Pocahontas. The chiefs on the floats were attired in white with white feathers. The scenes with the wigwams and campfires were very interesting and real.

The procession was an hour in passing a given point. The New Year clubs, in their fantastic costumes, added much to the display, and so many appearing in succession gave one a little idea of what the effect would be if all the clubs united in one procession on January 1.

A grand display of fireworks in the park ended the demonstration.

And so Penn Treaty Park was officially opened. From that day, October 28, 1893, to the present, there has never been another such demonstration to match it!

CHAPTER 4

PENN TREATY PARK

The First Sixty Years, 1893 to 1953

In 1893, when Penn Treaty Park first opened, Mr. Henry Conan Merritt (1844–1917) was selected to be its first park superintendent. Merritt lived at 441 Allen Street for just about all of his seventy-three years. He was the son of Thomas and Sarah Merritt, longtime residents of Kensington who had five children, with Henry the middle child. His father was a wharf builder, and Henry followed his father into that line of work. Once Penn Treaty Park opened in 1893, and with Henry getting up in years (he was just about fifty when the park opened), he probably welcomed a less strenuous occupation. It is said that with "only a nightstick, he single-handedly patrolled the park and kept the peace."

When the City of Philadelphia decided to expand Delaware Avenue, it bought up all the properties on Merritt's block of Allen Street, except for his family's house, which was spared, as fate would have it. The family did, however, lose a small piece of the property to the expansion.

Henry C. Merritt died at his Allen Street home on February 8, 1917, at the age of seventy-three. His obituary listed members of the following organizations as welcome to attend his funeral, which presumably means he was a member of these groups: Mount Moriah Lodge No. 155 of the Free and Associated Masons; the Kensington RAC No. 253; Kensington Commandery, No. 54, Knight's Templars; Masonic Veterans' Association; Captain John Taylor Temple, No. 24: O of UA; Stonemen's Fellowship Club; and Superintendents of City Parks. His body was to be interred at North Cedar Hills.

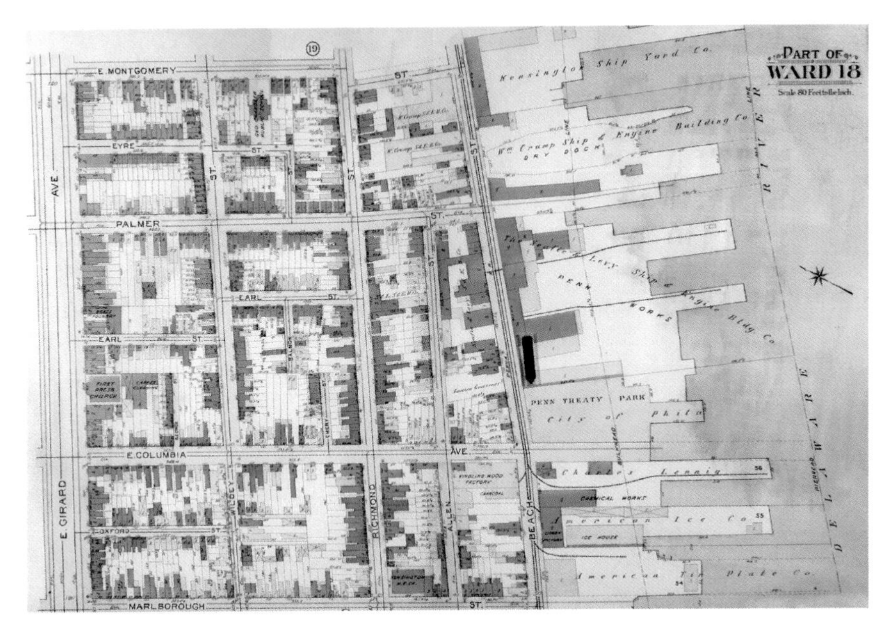

A map showing Penn Treaty Park and the surrounding neighborhood before the city brought Delaware Avenue through and before the construction of Interstate 95, dated 1904. *Courtesy of the author.*

Penn Treaty Park on April 16, 1910. The original fountain is shown in the center of the park. *Courtesy Philadelphia City Archives.*

During Merritt's tenure as park superintendent, many residents of the neighborhood enjoyed the park and the events held there, including free band concerts. Some old-time Fishtowners remember having these band concerts in the park as late as the early 1950s. Organizations like the Eighteenth Ward Republican Club, the Palmer Social Club and the Bramble Club provided free ice cream for children.

One unusual event that took place during Merritt's term as Penn Treaty Park superintendent happened in the year 1910. The U.S. Department of Commerce and Labor appropriated $250,000 to build a new immigration station in Philadelphia to replace the "ramshackle building" that was "overcrowded and insanitary." The secretary of the Department of Commerce and Labor selected a site next to Penn Treaty Park, where an old shipyard had been located but was now in ruins. This was Reaney Neafie and Company, later Neafie and Levy Shipyard, the place were Philadelphia Electric Company (PECO) would later build its plant in 1920.

The residents of the neighborhood complained that an immigration station would be a blight on historic Penn Treaty Park and that the new immigrants would wind up hanging out in their park. There was still a bit of the nativist spirit in the local population, held over from the days of May 1844, when Fishtown was a hotbed for Nativist Party sympathies.

Shipping men pointed out the value that the station would have to the port of Philadelphia, and several public-spirited citizens argued that the Penn Treaty Park would be a symbol of patriotism for the arriving immigrants who would soon become citizens.

Apparently, from 1907 to 1911, Penn Treaty's Pier 57 was used as a drop-off point for newly arrived immigrants who were being registered at the Gloucester, New Jersey facility. Some thought that building a new station in this area of town would not be met with opposition. They were wrong.

While the factions were contending, Philadelphia's mayor John Edger Reyburn declared that he would not grant a permit to the government to build the station. "We don't want it anyhow," he said. "An immigration station is an annoyance." The mayor refused to help find a better site in an acceptable location. A quarter of a million dollars (in 1910 dollars) was lost to Philadelphia when the station was built on the Jersey side of the river. It would not be the last time that Kensingtonians would reject plans to build near "their" Penn Treaty Park; similar opposition arose in 2007 when SugarHouse Casino proposed to build a slot parlor just south of the park.

Surveys and plans exist for this time period for a proposed two-story commercial and recreational pier. The lower deck of the pier was to have a

A proposed idea for a two-story commercial and recreation pier at Penn Treaty Park, 1916. This plan was never carried out. *Courtesy Philadelphia City Archives.*

wharfinger's office, stevedore's toilets, boiler room and coal storage. There were going to be twenty-foot-long bays on the north and south sides of the first floor of the pier, with thirteen different bays on each side.

While the pier looked great and might have been a commercial and recreational success, as it also included rail lines that ran right into it, it was never built. The speculation at the time was that the pier was never really going to be built. The pier was to be built close to the northern border of the park and built in such a way that there would not be enough water space, as was required by law, between this new pier and the proposed pier of the Department of Commerce and Labor, thus helping to nullify the immigration pier plans.

Once the U.S. Department of Commerce and Labor decided not to build their pier next to Penn Treaty Park, the plans for a proposed two-story commercial and recreation pier for Penn Treaty Park were also scrapped. After winning this battle, park enthusiasts then wanted the city to purchase the Neafie and Levy site and expand the park northwards. These plans apparently never escalated.

Pier 57 in Penn Treaty Park in 1912, before the reconstruction of a bulkhead and the creation of the new pier in 1920. *Courtesy Philadelphia City Archives.*

During this immigration pier controversy, Lady Eileen Knox, daughter of Lord Ranfurly and a descendant of William Penn, once visited the Penn Treaty Park memorial. Lady Knox helped to carry the train of Queen Mary during the coronation of King George and Queen Mary in 1911.

A couple of years later, surveys of September 3, 1917, were completed that showed the original open-frame pavilion that sat at the end of the park near the water, before any pier was built out into the river. This pavilion measured forty feet square and sat about twelve feet from the bulkhead wall. At this time, there was also a wooden-frame police station at the foot of Columbia Avenue on the north side and a boat landing that used to be at the northeast corner of the park's shoreline but was already being replaced by an iron fence.

When Penn Treaty Park was first established, it was under the jurisdiction of the Bureau of City Property. From recorded accounts, it would appear that the bureau did little in the way of caring for the park, and the job fell to local residents who came together to help keep the park clean and enjoyable. When the park was created, there were still homes on Beach Street, but after

Delaware Avenue was built and later expanded, many of these homes were demolished or gave way to factories and other commercial ventures. The park became detached from the neighborhood, even more so once Interstate 95 was built in the early 1960s.

Reports show that after only twenty years of existence, the park was already showing signs of falling into disrepair and was described by one as a "dirty hole," a place were "several parents forbade their kids to go." The park's downward trend coincided with the death of its first superintendent, Henry C. Merritt, in 1917.

The city did not appear to do much upkeep of the park during its first twenty-five years. Adequate lighting was not installed until the 1930s. After Philadelphia Electric Company's building was erected on the old Neafie and Levy Shipyard property to the north of the park in 1920, the huge PECO sign from the south side of the plant illuminated the park and discouraged the young couples who were making a "lover's lane" out of the place. It was also about this time when PECO erected the iron fence between its property and Penn Treaty Park.

Thinking that the park had no caretakers, PECO even tried to have the Penn Treaty Pier demolished so that the coal barges delivering to its plant would have any easier time of it. However, the local residents' spirit was still alive—the attempt was rejected and efforts were made to renovate the park.

A wholly new pier was built in 1920 and later used for harbor police and fire units. Along with the new pier, the bulkheads at the foot of Columbia Avenue and across the whole riverside of the park were rebuilt.

The earlier plans from 1917 appear to have called for a total re-greening of the park, with all areas to be graded, sodded and seeded. A playground with a framed toilet facilities building was shown to be planned for the park. New pavements and foot walks were also in the works. The park was only twenty-four years old and already it was going through its first major renovation, a scene that would be repeated every quarter of a century.

During this period of renovation, the park was being touted as a place to visit. Perhaps it was the sesquicentennial celebrations (in 1926) that prompted city officials to renovate the park, as various publications promoting the sesquicentennial mentioned it as a place that would be sure to get its fair share of tourists during the event. The American Legionnaires' Eighth Annual National Convention met in Philadelphia October 11–15, 1926, and in an article published in the *Oxford Junction* (Oxford, Iowa) the Penn Treaty Monument was listed as a place of interest when visiting Philadelphia.

A view from the south of Pier 57 in Penn Treaty Park, showing construction in 1919. *Courtesy Philadelphia City Archives.*

A view of a bulkhead at the foot of Columbia Avenue and Pier 57, showing work completed as of January 20, 1920. *Courtesy Philadelphia City Archives.*

Pier 57 North in Penn Treaty Park, under construction, March 18, 1920. *Courtesy Philadelphia City Archives.*

The removal of the old bulkhead at the foot of Columbia Avenue, August 3, 1920. *Courtesy Philadelphia City Archives.*

The park's popularity can be also be seen by earlier accounts of writers and the publicity it got from the press of major publishers in America and elsewhere. Rand McNally's *Handy Guide to Philadelphia and Environs* published in 1896 included a bit on the newly created Penn Treaty Park, stating that it was in "good condition with pretty appointments" and opened on July 4, 1893, "with imposing ceremonies." The eleventh edition of the *Encylopaedia Britannica* (1911), considered by many to be the most scholarly edition, included in its article on Philadelphia a mention of the new Penn Treaty Park. Christopher Morley included the park in his *Travels in Philadelphia*, published in 1920, as did Clifford Johnson in his book *What to See in America* (1922), which included Penn Treaty Park as a tourist destination.

Starting in about 1911, or slightly earlier, Penn Treaty Pier (Pier 57) became the home of a unit of the harbor police. The *William S. Stokley*, a harbor police boat, was stationed at the foot of Columbia Avenue. It was one of four harbor police boats. The boat made almost daily trips conveying prisoners to the Philadelphia House of Correction, or taking sick inmates from the house of correction to Philadelphia Hospital, as well as other special trips and duties.

Pier 57 North in Penn Treaty Park, inshore side and north side, showing newly constructed pier and pavilion, August 3, 1920. *Courtesy Philadelphia City Archives.*

A plaque attached to the gate of the new pier in 1920, displaying that contractors Simpson and Brown built the pier. *Courtesy Philadelphia City Archives.*

Around 1911–12, the Patrol Launch *Margaret*, one of Philadelphia's two Patrol Launches, was also stationed at Penn Treaty Park, and at one point the merchant marines also had a training ship, the *Annapolis*, that docked at Pier 57.

On June 7, 1931, the park made the news when a boat from this unit of the harbor police exploded at the foot of Columbia Avenue. The superintendent of police, William B. Mills, and six harbor policemen were hurt. The boat, named for the superintendent, was on a trial trip and exploded as it pulled into Penn Treaty Park. After a little more than two decades, the harbor police and fire units were relocated.

A "lighting survey" plan executed on February 23, 1933, shows that park officials were planning to install lighting for the first time. The 1933 survey shows plans to install seven double-light poles along the north side of the park, six single-light poles within the park itself, two lights on the pier under the pavilion and another two lights on the pier not under the pavilion. Two

Over the years, the community has often come together to reenact Penn's Treaty and keep its memory alive, circa 1932. *Courtesy John Connors Collection.*

other light poles were to be placed on the street—one on Columbia Avenue and one on Beach Street.

About this time, the Boy Scouts of America's plaque was erected, which still rests in the park. It commemorates a tree planting.

MILES LEDERER AND THE TRANSFER OF PENN TREATY PARK FROM THE BUREAU OF RECREATION TO THE FAIRMOUNT PARK COMMISSION

In the late 1940s and early 1950s, Miles Lederer became another in a long line of public-spirited citizens who made it part of their life's work to secure the preservation of honoring Penn's Treaty.

Lederer was born in Philadelphia on December 30, 1897. Born Myer Lederer, he was the son of Samuel Lederer and Minerva Shartzwald and the grandson of Moritz Lederer, a Jewish shopkeeper from Austria who came to America in 1876 and settled in the Northern Liberties neighborhood of Philadelphia, just south of Fishtown. Moritz and his wife Anna had at least nine children. Samuel, being their eldest son, followed his father into shopkeeping.

At the outbreak of World War I, Miles Lederer joined the military and served overseas. He also married about this time. Raised Jewish by his father, Miles Lederer married Susan Scullin, an Irish Catholic from Fishtown. Father Murphy at St. Michael's is the one responsible for Lederer's conversion to Roman Catholicism. Miles and Susan's family would eventually include eleven children.

The 1920 census has Miles and his family living at 1222 Day Street, with Miles working as a lighthouse service machinist, but by 1930 Miles had moved his family to 1205 Frankford Avenue near Girard Avenue in a twenty-dollars-per-month rental home. By the time his son (also named Miles) was reported wounded in World War II, Miles had moved his family again, this time to 1231 Shackamaxon Street, the house that would become the family home and where some members of the Lederer family still live today.

In 1930, Miles worked as a machinist in a shipyard, but by the mid-1930s he was working as a laborer at Andy's Café on Frankford Avenue. Andy's Café today is supposed to be Johnny Brenda's at Frankford and Girard.

Miles Lederer eventually went to a business college and became involved in the Democratic Party at a time when the Republicans dominated Philadelphia. He became a local Eighteenth Ward Democratic committeeman and eventually the ward's chairman. He also began to take an active role in the community, helping to organize the Shackamaxon Boys Club. His education and involvement in politics helped him to land a job with the Department of Auditor General, where he was an auditor-investigator for twelve years before being elected in 1948 from the Eleventh District to serve in the Pennsylvania House of Representatives.

Lederer, a World War I veteran, was elected to the house seat that was held by a popular, decorated World War I veteran and Girard Avenue funeral director, a man by the name of William Rowen. Lederer and Rowen were both members in the American Legion's Elm Tree Post 88, the VFW club now located on Palmer Street. Rowen, a Republican, was awarded a Purple Heart and a Victory Medal during the war. He was wounded and lay hidden on the battlefield for two days before being able to get medical attention. His wounds became infected, causing a long illness. Rowen's uncle, also named William Rowen, was mentioned previously in this book as the one who was instrumental in the founding of Penn Treaty Park. As president of the Bramble Club, he had led the park's opening day ceremonies back in 1893.

Old, worn, frame police station at the foot of Columbia Avenue, with the comfort station in the background, March 1954. *Courtesy Fairmount Park Historic Resource Archive.*

The park's pier and pavilion in decline—the bronze plaque is missing and the tall flagpoles are now gone, circa 1954. *Courtesy Fairmount Park Historic Resource Archive.*

During his legislative career, Lederer was a friend to police, firemen, veterans and government employees of first- and second-class cities, often introducing bills in the house, or reporting on bills introduced into the house, that favored better conditions and treatments for these civil service workers, first responders and veterans of foreign wars. He also made it a special point to advocate for the care of Penn Treaty Park.

During Lederer's six years (1949–53) as a state legislator, the Pennsylvania Statehouse did not meet every year the way it does now. There were no legislative sessions in the years 1948, 1950 or 1952, thus Lederer's actions as a state representative were limited to those years that the house was in session: 1949, 1951 and 1953.

In the years immediately following World War II, local Fishtown residents, including Lederer, once more turned their attention to cleaning up and restoring Penn Treaty Park. Led by the Eighteenth Ward Community Council, a forerunner to the Fishtown Civic Association, which preceded the Fishtown Neighbors Association, the activists felt that the only way the park would get the attention it deserved would be to have the park transferred to the Fairmount Park Commission. The issue was introduced to the city council, but council transferred the park from the Bureau of City Property to the Bureau of Recreation.

Lederer's first action to help Penn Treaty Park was on March 15, 1949, when he introduced House Bill No. 1249, "An act making appropriations to the City of Philadelphia for repairing Penn Treaty Monument, and improving the grounds thereof, located in the 18th Ward of said City of Philadelphia." However, the bill was referred to the committee on appropriations and there it remained for another month.

On April 6, 1949, Lederer addressed the Pennsylvania Statehouse regarding Bill No. 1249 and asked for it to be read out of committee. His address to the Pennsylvania House gave a glimpse of the history of Bill No. 1249. Lederer stated that on February 7, 1949, the members of the community council of the Eighteenth Ward, together with its president Mr. William Rowen Grant, requested Lederer to introduce a bill in the House of Representatives for the purpose of making an appropriation to the City of Philadelphia for the repairs to the Penn Treaty Monument and improvements to the grounds surrounding it. That bill (No. 1249) was introduced in the house and was immediately sent to committee for review.

However, Lederer did not want the bill to die in committee and thus addressed the house, giving them a brief history of Penn's Treaty, the park and how the present (1949) condition of the park jeopardized this honored place:

> *Penn Treaty Park, in which this monument is located has become extremely run down, the walks broken and the grass completely trampled out, the rest rooms boarded up and the benches and the drinking fountain have disappeared completely. The iron fence used to protect the children by being a barrier between them and the river is in such broken condition that a repetition of death at that spot is quite possible.*

Lederer continued his address about the importance of the park to Pennsylvania's history. He then asked the Pennsylvania House to appropriate at least $50,000 to restore the park and to read his bill out of committee. Lederer told the statehouse that only recently, on March 16, 1949, Philadelphia newspapers reported on Bill No. 1249, the condition of Penn Treaty Park and the fact that the community's hopes of having the park transferred to the Fairmount Park Commission were dashed when the City of Philadelphia transferred the park from the hands of the Bureau of City Property to the Bureau of Recreation. This would put the park under the care of a city department that, in all likelihood, would make the park just another playground instead of a place that kept the focus on honoring

Penn's Treaty. Lederer placed the blame for the park being transferred to the Bureau of Recreation on Philadelphia councilman Phineas Green, who hailed from the Northern Liberties neighborhood and not Kensington's (Fishtown's) Eighteenth Ward, where Penn Treaty Park was located.

State Representative Lederer also challenged the statehouse on why Penn Treaty Park was not included in the "catalog of Historical sites and remains in Pennsylvania" (as of March 1949) and speculated that it was not included because the state was "ashamed to view this park in the condition that it was in at the present time." He went on to mention that in the very chamber of the Pennsylvania House of Representatives was a large painting of "that famous treaty made under the old elm tree in the village of Shackamaxon on the Delaware." He urged the statehouse to read his bill out of committee.

Lederer's actions were heard across America, as witnessed by the following report in a Bismarck, North Dakota newspaper, the *Bismarck Tribune*, on March 15, 1949:

> *A Pennsylvania lawmaker says the misuse that has befallen the William Penn Treaty monument in Philadelphia shouldn't happen to an historic shrine. State Representative Miles W. Lederer, Philadelphia Democrat, told the legislature Monday: "The monument (marking the spot where Penn signed a treaty with the Indians in 1682) has become dilapidated and is rapidly falling into decay. The Penn Treaty Park on which the monument is situated has become extremely rundown, the grass completely trampled out, the drinking fountain has disappeared, the restrooms are boarded up, the benches have disappeared, the automobiles park and drive all over the park and the iron fence used to protect children from falling into the Delaware river is in a broken condition." Lederer asked that Philadelphia be given $50,000 to restore the park.*

This story also ran in papers in Oakland, California; St. Joseph, Missouri; and Lowell, Massachusetts, amongst others. While Lederer's address was impressive, his efforts seem to have landed on deaf ears in the statehouse. Lederer's House Bill No. 1249 remained in the committee on appropriations, where it was never read out and thus died.

During this time, while Miles Lederer was calling for the restoration of Penn Treaty Park, one of the local Philadelphia newspapers started to pick up on the story. Paul Jones, who wrote a column called "Candid Shots," mentioned visiting the park in its dilapidated condition:

> *A low concrete marker, with metal tablet, is set into the ground under a youthful elm tree, planted by the Boy Scouts in 1932. This was to replace the great elm tree, blown over by the wind in 1810…An old settler was sitting on a bench, looking out over the river and smoking his pipe…*[we] *joined him. "This place is a disgrace," he told us, "and nobody will do anything about it. Miles Lederer, at Harrisburg, and Phinnie Green in City Council, they both tried. But it didn't do any good. Lederer's got a couple of bills before the Legislature right now. Bet you 10 to 1 nothing's ever done about it…You ever been in Washington Square? You know how nice it looks? Well, that's the way Penn Treaty was, forty, fifty years ago. A fountain, flowers, calla lilies, tulips, walks all neat, not busted down the way they are now, plenty of benches, and people that behave themselves. There was a man here that carried a big bullwhip. Any kid that got out of line got a touch of the whip. If that didn't stop him, the cops would arrest him…They boarded up that comfort station nine, ten years ago," he went on pointing with his pipe stem. "Said they were going to fix it. Haven't done a tap on it since."*

The old-timer in the column went on to say:

> *The City owned the park, first it was the Bureau of City Properties, they didn't do much repair, and proceeded to turn it over to the Bureau of Recreation, in about 1948. Now the Fairmount Park Commission was to take it over. In typical bureaucrat fashion, some folks from the city came out with all sorts of plans on what was to be restored, had a photo op, and then went away never to be seen or heard from again.*

The writer finished his column by stating that it was a good thing that Penn Treaty Park was hard to find, otherwise he wasn't sure what tourists would think of us!

Thwarted by the death of Bill No. 1249 in committee and still fearful that the park would be relegated to just another playground under the Bureau of Recreation and lose its historical significance, Miles Lederer introduced Resolution No. 53 to the statehouse on June 6, 1951, calling upon the City of Philadelphia "to take measures for the proper care and development of the Penn Treaty Park," and that the city "should without delay carry out its responsibility for the proper care and improvement of the Penn Treaty Park, which is a property of the City." The resolution was referred to the committee on rules, where it also proceeded to die.

Not one to give up, Lederer, still during the legislative session of 1951, then introduced to the statehouse Bills No. 603 and No. 735. Bill No. 603 was to allocate money to the City of Philadelphia to care for the park. This bill died in committee. Bill No. 735 was a different tactic tried by Lederer. In this bill, he tried to get the state to take over the park. The bill's title was, "An act authorizing the Pennsylvania Historical Commission, on behalf of the Commonwealth of Pennsylvania, to acquire by gift or purchase Penn Treaty Park, from the City of Philadelphia, providing for the control, management, supervising, restoration, improvement and maintenance thereof, and making an appropriation." This bill would have the State of Pennsylvania take control of Penn Treaty Park and make it a state historical site. As with all of his previous attempts to restore and improve Penn Treaty Park, Bill No. 735 was also thwarted when it was referred to the committee of appropriations, where it eventually died.

While Lederer may have come to a dead end in the statehouse, he kept up the fight. The Eighteenth Ward Community Council petitioned the Fairmount Park Commission to assume control of the park. Lederer solicited the help of Park Commission member John B. Kelly Jr. to lend his support. Kelly was helpful in getting the Park Commission to agree to take over Penn Treaty Park, but the commission was on a tight budget, one that was regulated by the state legislature at that time. Lederer went to work in Harrisburg and introduced Bill No. 612 into the statehouse, which made "appropriations to the Fairmount Park Commission of Philadelphia for repairing the Monument and improving the grounds of the Penn Treaty Monument." With the help of others, Lederer was able to secure a $75,000 allotment to be placed in the Fairmount Park Commission budget for the permanent care of Penn Treaty Park—thus, after several years of fighting in the statehouse and with the Philadelphia City Council, Penn Treaty Park was transferred from the Bureau of Recreation to the Fairmount Park Commission in 1954, where it remains in its care to the present day.

The hard work of the Eighteenth Ward Community Council and State Representative Miles Lederer paid off. The Fairmount Park Commission's annual report of 1954 stated that Penn Treaty Park would be restored with funds provided in the capital improvement program. The report went on to state that the newly acquired park had been "sadly neglected over the years and required grading, new walks, and a complete planting." The eventual restoration of the park included the planting of 10 English yews, 100 barberries and 1,400 ground cover plants.Two trees, an American elm and an American holly, were also planted. The park also soon saw the restoration of the public restrooms and drinking fountain, and there was the addition of an officer of the Fairmount Park Police who patrolled the park.

Miles Lederer died in office on December 25, 1953, after having served as a Pennsylvania State Representative for Philadelphia's Eleventh District (at that time) for a short six years. Today, Fishtown has honored State Representative Lederer by naming the Fishtown Recreation Complex's public swimming pool after him.

Miles Lederer and his wife Susan raised eleven children, with many of them going on to distinguished careers. Several of the children followed their father into politics. In 1962, William J. Lederer (1923–2008) was elected as a Democrat to the Pennsylvania State Representative seat once held by his father (now renamed the 175th District). He gave up his seat in the statehouse to become a judge on the Court of Common Pleas of Philadelphia. At the time of his death, he was a senior judge of the Commonwealth Appeal Court in Pennsylvania.

Another of Miles Lederer's sons was Raymond Lederer, born in 1938, who took over his brother's Pennsylvania State Representative seat when William J. Lederer became a judge. He later gave up the seat to become a Democratic member of the United States House of Representatives, representing Pennsylvania's Third Congressional District from 1977 to 1981.

Judge William J. Lederer's wife, Marie Panosetti Lederer, was elected to the seat once held by her husband, brother-in-law and father-in-law. She served as a Pennsylvania state representative from 1994 to 2006.

Another of Miles Lederer's sons—his namesake, Miles "Doll" Lederer—was a onetime business manager and president of the American Federation of Labor–Congress of Industrial Organizations Local 161, Riggers and Machinery Movers union. He was a decorated World War II veteran, having served on the *Charles Carroll* in the South Pacific and received the Silver Star, the Legion of Merit and the Purple Heart. The *Charles Carroll* was described by war correspondent Ernie Pyle as "one of the fightingest ships of the emergency Navy."

And still another son, Francis J. Lederer, eventually became the chief of Philadelphia County Detectives and the executive director of the Philadelphia County and State Detectives Association of Pennsylvania.

In total, the Lederer family, with their long years of service to Philadelphia, is a family that all Kensingtonians and Fishtowners can be proud of.

CHAPTER 5

THE BICENTENNIAL, TERCENTENARY AND THE PARK EXPANSION, 1954 TO 2008

During the decades of 1960s and early 1970s, as America's economy began to change and manufacturers started to move overseas or relocate to the South, a number of businesses and industries began to vacate Fishtown's waterfront. This process created a sense of isolation in that part of the neighborhood, which was impacted by Interstate 95 bulldozing its way through the neighborhood in the 1960s. The new highway literally cut off Penn Treaty Park and the waterfront from the neighborhood; except for a few blocks of houses along Allen Street and parts of Richmond Street, Penn Treaty Park was barely visible to the community.

Delaware Avenue had earlier been widened and ran between the neighborhood and the park. The road was a jumble of old railroad tracks, Belgian block paving stones and too many potholes to count. Most people tried their best to avoid it, only driving on it if absolutely necessary. The park was shadowed and obscured by PECO's expanded generating plant, American Can Company, Warner Company's warehouses, Penn Atlantic's Millworks and a Mobil Gas Station, as well as other decrepit old buildings falling into disrepair.

Local juvenile delinquents in the neighborhood started to make their way back into the park. The patrolman's watch—reinitiated in the 1950s when the Fairmount Park Commission first took over the care of the park—was disbanded for some reason in the early 1970s. Soon the park again became a "lover's lane" for romantics at night and a general all-around hangout for

Old railroad tracks and potholes along Beach Street, fronting Penn Treaty Park, dated June 16, 1980. *Courtesy Fairmount Park Historic Resource Archive.*

Mobil Gas Station before demolition, circa 1980. This is the site where Haozous's *Penn's Treaty* sculpture sits today. *Courtesy Fairmount Park Historic Resource Archive.*

A view of Penn Treaty Park from the Delaware River before the park was expanded, July 13, 1980. *Courtesy Fairmount Park Historic Resource Archive.*

A view of the park facing east from Columbia and Delaware Avenues, showing how the park had become hidden by industrial development, circa 1955. *Courtesy Philadelphia City Archives.*

idle youths, a place for young and old to drink beer and generally trash the area. Youths again began to use the treaty monument for target practice when throwing rocks.

THE BICENTENNIAL AND SIGNS OF RENOVATION

The community's attachment to the park would not die. As the American Bicentennial (1976) approached, the Fishtown Civic Association and the Kensington Community Council worked to have the park renovated.

The Fishtown Civic Association was a rather new neighborhood group. Founded in the mid- to late 1960s, the group came into existence as contractors were making their way through the neighborhood building Interstate 95. Blocks of homes and business was taken down, and unlike the Society Hill and Queen's Village neighborhoods, Fishtown did not receive any fancy landscaping.

The Kensington Community Council dated back to 1939 and met regularly on topics that addressed the state of the neighborhood. A longtime

The brick comfort station in ruins—spray-painted and destroyed by neighborhood vandals, May 16, 1975. *Courtesy Fairmount Park Historic Resource Archive.*

A Penn Treaty Park pier in disrepair, fenced off, later to be demolished for good, May 16, 1975. *Courtesy Fairmount Park Historic Resource Archive.*

member of the group was Henry C. Kreiss (1910–1990). In 1917, Henry C. Kreiss was only seven years old when he first visited Penn Treaty Park. He and his seven sisters would take the ship *Elizabeth Smith* to Red Bank, New Jersey, otherwise known as "Soupy Island," for their free bowl of soup, milk and cookies. Soupy Island is a place that brings a smile to most of the old-timers in Fishtown, as almost everyone took the boat to Soupy Island.

That first year (1917) that Kreiss visited Penn Treaty Park was a mere twenty-four years after the park was founded and the same year that marked the death of the first park superintendent, Henry C. Merritt. It could be said that old Merritt passed the torch for the care of the park to the young and impressionable Henry C. Kreiss, and when Kreiss was too old to care for the park, he passed the torch to another young and impressionable man by the name of John Connors, about whom we will read more later in this chapter.

In time Kreiss would marry and have his own family, often bringing them to Penn Treaty Park. In 1941, Kreiss joined the Kensington Community Council and fought for the care of Penn Treaty Park up until his dying days in 1990, serving almost a full fifty years as a steward of Penn Treaty Park.

Mr. Kreiss was nicknamed "Mr. Kensington" due to his love of the community and his active participation in its promotion and upkeep. Kreiss

Henry C. "Mr. Kensington" Kreiss (1910–1990) was a leading advocate to have the Fairmount Park Commission take control of park, 1982. *Courtesy John Connors Collection.*

PROPOSAL: THE EXPANSION AND DEVELOPMENT OF
PENN TREATY PARK, KENSINGTON,
PHILADELPHIA, PA

(For the Opening of Space for Recreation, and for Community Service, as a Memorial to WILLIAM PENN, his Treaty of Friendship with the Indians, and the Implementation of his Concept of Social Justice.)

This proposal requires the extension of the present PENN TREATY PARK grounds in a westerly direction along the bank of the Delaware River (toward the Benjamin Franklin Bridge), to implement the following plan:

The area, cleared of present buildings, should be developed with the reconstruction of FAIRMAN'S MANSION or some comparable building, a large parking lot to accommodate buses and cars, and benches along the river front for public recreation.

The mansion should house a museum where artifacts or reproductions pertaining to William Penn's dealings with the Indians could be displayed. These realia might include personal possessions of William Penn, memorabilia made from the treaty elm which fell during a storm on March 3, 1810; originals or copies of paintings commemorating the treaty spot, and Indian relics of every description.

The temperature-controlled building should house a lecture room capable of seating 150 to 200 people. Here, with musical background and narrated slides, the account of Penn's meeting with Indians at Shackamaxon could be presented to groups of students, tourists, and other visitors to the park.

Lavatory facilities for men and women as well as drinking water should be provided.

The plans should include living quarters for a full-time caretaker and a ship where prints, color slides, reproductions of Indian and Penn artifacts and related brochures and books could be sold to assist with the financial upkeep of the building.

Because of its isolated location on the river front, it is possible that consideration should be given to walling the entire compound for security purposes.

The Philadelphia Electric Company's transformers should be removed from their present position in front of the park.

Directional signs to the park should be posted at advantageous locations on nearby streets and highways, including the new and nearby Delaware Expressway #95.

Dr. Etta M. Pettyjohn

Dr. Etta May Pettyjohn's proposal for a Penn Treaty Museum, offered during a talk given in June 1970 to the Kensington Community Council. *Courtesy John Connors Collection.*

was very instrumental in helping to preserve Penn Treaty Park, acting as one of the main advocates to have the Fairmount Park Commission take it over back in the early 1950s.

Another supporter of the park and a colleague of Kreiss's in his efforts to renovate and promote Penn Treaty Park was Dr. Etta May Pettyjohn (1909–2005). Pettyjohn was the daughter of Theodore T. Pettyjohn, a longtime Fishtown tugboat captain, and his wife, Alma B. Pepper. Dr. Pettyjohn's parents, originally from Delaware, moved to Philadelphia and lived for a time in several different homes on the 800 block of East Thompson Street, where Dr. Pettyjohn was born. She graduated from Kensington High School for Girls in 1925, and three decades later (after getting her bachelor's, master's and doctoral degrees all from the University of Pennsylvania) returned to Kensington High School as its principal (1956–71). After her retirement, she used her energies to support the Kensington Community Council and the Fishtown Civic Association. She was the driving force behind the restoration of Penn Treaty Park.

In June 1970, Dr. Pettyjohn gave a talk to the Kensington Community Council titled "The History of the Park with Recommendations for Its Use and Rehabilitation for the Bicentennial." In her address, Pettyjohn allowed the community to dream of a day when Penn Treaty Park would have its own interpretive museum. In a memo, she outlined her proposal for the Penn Treaty Museum:

> *Proposal: The Expansion and Development of Penn Treaty Park, Kensington, Philadelphia, PA.*
>
> *(For the Opening of Space for Recreation, and for Community service, as a Memorial to William Penn, his Treaty of Friendship with the Indians, and the Implementation of his Concept of Social Justice.)*
>
> *This proposal requires the extension of the present Penn Treaty Park grounds in a westerly direction along the bank of the Delaware River (toward the Benjamin Franklin Bridge), to implement the following plan:*
>
> *The area, cleared of present buildings, should be developed with the reconstruction of Fairman's Mansion or some comparable building, a large parking lot to accommodate buses and cars, and benches along the river front for public recreation.*
>
> *The mansion should house a museum where artifacts or reproductions pertaining to William Penn's dealings with the Indians could be displayed. These realia might include personal possessions of William Penn, memorabilia made from the treaty elm which fell during a storm on*

March 3 [actually March 5], *1810; originals or copies of paintings commemorating the treaty spot, and Indian relics of every description.*

The temperature-controlled building should house a lecture room capable of seating 150 to 200 people. Here, with musical background and narrated slides, the account of Penn's meeting with Indians at Shackamaxon could be presented to groups of students, tourists, and other visitors to the park.

Lavatory facilities for men and women as well as drinking water should be provided.

The plans should include living quarters for a full-time caretaker and a shop where prints, color slides, reproductions of Indian and Penn artifacts and related brochures and books could be sold to assist with the financial upkeep of the buildings.

Because of its isolated location on the river front, it is possible that consideration should be given to walling the entire compound for security purposes.

The Philadelphia Electric Company's transformers should be removed from their present position in front of the park.

Directional signs to the park should be posted at advantageous locations on nearby streets and highways, including the new and nearby Delaware Expressway #95.

Dr. Pettyjohn's dreams for Penn Treaty Park, then, seemed to fit in with precisely the type of development being sought for Philadelphia's waterfront. This time during the buildup toward the bicentennial celebration was an ideal time to share Penn Treaty Park with the rest of the world.

The first signs that Penn Treaty Park was going to receive another overhaul were in the annual report of the Fairmount Park Commission, dated 1976–77. In that report it is stated that Penn Treaty Park was to be completely rehabilitated, including new walkways, sitting areas, fencing, lighting and landscaping. The next year's report (1977–78) showed that $238,000 was spent on renovating the park. Of this amount, $223,000 was federal money from the EDA (Economic Development Administration) and $15,000 was from the City of Philadelphia. Besides the renovations mentioned in the 1976–77 report, the 1977–78 report also mentions that the "monument" would be relocated.

While Dr. Pettyjohn's museum was never built, there were some extensive renovations made to the park. In preparation for the bicentennial, old Pier 57—in disrepair and no longer used except for fishing or by kids dangerously diving into the river—was finally removed. Plans for the original Penn Society's Treaty Monument to be moved from the northwest corner of the park to an area closer to the center of the park were made and carried out either in late 1978 or soon after.

Oddly enough, the bicentennial was also the time that Penn Treaty Park was finally awarded a Pennsylvania State Marker through the Pennsylvania Historical and Museum Commission (PHMC). The program had been in operation since 1914, but for some reason the good folks in Harrisburg never saw the need to mark the founding place of Pennsylvania. It took PHMC sixty-three years to finally notice that there was a place called Penn Treaty Park and that it was the place where William Penn made a Treaty of Amity and Friendship with the American Indians, which started the founding of Pennsylvania.

TERCENTENARY CELEBRATIONS AND THE EXPANSION OF THE PARK

Much like how the return of Lafayette in 1824 instilled a historic pride in people like Roberts Vaux, John F. Watson and Pierre S. du Ponceau, the upcoming tercentenary celebrations of the state of Pennsylvania instilled a boost to the historic memory of the community and the city as a whole.

In 1978, after the bicentennial celebrations had died down, the Fishtown Civic Association eyed the year 1982, the 300th anniversary of Penn's Treaty, as the year when the park would hopefully receive further renovation. The date was also the tercentenary anniversary for the state of Pennsylvania. The bicentennial renovation renewed the fighting spirit in Fishtown and, again, the Fishtown Civic Association and the Kensington Community Council, as well as other concerned citizens, led the charge not only to further restore the park, but now also to finally expand it. The groups decided to form a Penn Treaty Park Tercentenary Committee and invite anyone in the city of Philadelphia to join them. Besides the Fishtown Civic and the Kensington Council, some who took up the challenge were members of the American Society of Friends, the Fishtown Athletic Club, Elaine Peden ("the William Penn Lady"), the Potamkin family, former residents and a number of others from around the city.

The year 1982 was a special year because it marked Pennsylvania's tercentenary celebration. In conjunction with the yearlong events conducted by the city, various activities took place at Penn Treaty Park. The Daughters of the American Colonists commissioned Frank C. Gaylord, the sculptor of the Korean War Memorial in Washington, D.C., to carve a statue of William Penn.The statue of Penn was dedicated in park ceremonies in 1982 at the tercentenary celebrations. How Gaylord's sculpture made its way to Penn Treaty Park is an interesting story and is told in the sixth chapter of this book.

Another tercentenary celebration that took place at the park in 1982 was a William Penn Sabbath that was held on October 24, 1982, by the Lower Kensington Ecumenical Council and the members of the Fishtown Civic Association. After a processional rendition of the "Battle Hymn of the Republic" and the singing of "The Star-Spangled Banner," John Connors of the Fishtown Civic Association voiced the welcome and opening remarks. The Reverend Edward Cahill of Immaculate Conception RC Church gave the invocation for the day. There was silent prayer and words of assurance by Reverend Reinhard Kruse of Summerfield UM Church. Betty Quintavalle of the Lower Kensington Ecumenical Committee read the scripture along with James Winn of the Fishtown Civic Association. A First Presbyterian Church of Kensington minister, the Reverend Charles R. Schafer, held vesper prayer, and Kensington United Presbyterian Parish minister Reverend E. Bradford David gave an address: "William Penn—Man of Love." Henry

On Sunday, October 31, 1982, Native Americans in full regalia joined costumed Fishtowners for a reenactment of Penn's Treaty. *Courtesy John Connors Collection.*

Eastern Native American architecture and construction methods were demonstrated in the erection of a longhouse and two wigwams, circa 1982. *Courtesy John Connors Collection.*

The United American Indians of the Delaware Valley hosted a three-day powwow at the climax of a weeklong encampment at the park, circa 1982. *Courtesy John Connors Collection.*

C. Kreiss ("Mr. Kensington") read William Penn's Prayer for Philadelphia, which was followed by benediction given by the Reverend Robert Larson of Pilgrim Congregational. The program ended with "America the Beautiful" as the recessional.

The United American Indians of the Delaware Valley hosted a three-day powwow at the climax of a weeklong encampment in what is now the new section of Penn Treaty Park. Eastern Native American architecture and construction methods were demonstrated with the erection of a longhouse and two wigwams. The longhouse was the scene of traditional Indian worship services during the week and offered visitors a rare glance at the lifestyle that William Penn may have encountered. On Sunday, October 31, 1982, the American Indians, in full regalia, joined costumed Fishtowners for a reenactment of Penn's Treaty of Amity and Friendship, complete with an authentic replica of the wampum belt.

Fueled by a new generation of advocates for Penn Treaty Park and with the experiences of several generations before them, the Fishtown Civic Association, directed by Joe Torre, set about making the overhaul of Penn Treaty Park possible. Instead of Roberts Vaux, Pierre S. du Ponceau, Thomas S. Fernon and William Rowen, the new generation consisted of native Fishtowners and Kensingtonians like Dr. Etta May Pettyjohn, Henry C. Kreiss, Ruth Trauck, Sandy Salzman, Kathy Downey, Jim Weiss, Carol Smythe and Dorothy Sobotka, all of whom had a history of caring for the park.

John Connors, a newcomer to the neighborhood and a northeast Philadelphia transplant, was also caught up in the excitement of the park advocates. Connors, mentored by the likes of Kreiss and Pettyjohn, would go on to become one of the biggest Penn Treaty Park advocates and the founder of the virtual Penn Treaty Park Museum, an online museum that is his homage to Dr. Pettyjohn's 1970 speech calling for a Penn Treaty Park Museum. The website (www.penntreatymuseum.org) displays the history of Penn's Treaty and the park, as well as showcases Connors's collection of Penn's Treaty artifacts, prints and ephemera that he has assembled over the years.

THE TERCENTENARY COMMITTEE

In my correspondence with John Connors, the chairman of the tercentenary committee for the Fishtown Civic Association, Connors responded with an in-depth look at the history and activities of that committee. Since the committee played such an important role in the activities of the park during the tercentenary celebrations in 1982, as well as the park's expansion and rededication in 1987, I'll reproduce Connors's remarks in full:

> *In 1978, Jim Winn, President of the Fishtown Civic Association, encouraged John Connors to investigate the proposed PENNDOT plans to alter Delaware Avenue. It seemed there might be an opportunity to obtain some of the vacant industrial property along the Delaware River near Penn Treaty Park for additional recreational land for the community.*
>
> *The Fishtown Civic Association was a young organization with numerous issues to contend with, and the members were already involved in trying to address housing, zoning and crime. Who would want to work on a Delaware Avenue committee?*
>
> *The first contact was made with the Kensington Community Council. This established group had championed the upkeep of the park for many years and held annual meetings there. KCC was a respected organization with leaders from community schools, churches and businesses.*
>
> *Three people from KCC attended the first meeting of the exploratory group: Dr. Etta May Pettyjohn, Henry Kreiss and Ruth Trauck. With the addition of Fishtown Civic members Carol Smythe, Kathy Downey, Sharon Bezner, George Baker, Betty Quintavalle, Jim Weiss and Kay Welliver, a committee was born.*
>
> *Very quickly, the committee decided to expand its scope to include anyone with an interest in William Penn. Invitations were sent out to representatives of the American Society of Friends, and Beatrice Kirkbride and Dan Test responded. Beatrice Kirkbride, from the Society Hill area, brought an interest in historical preservation and Dan Test was a board member from Haverford College.*
>
> *Elaine Peden, the "William Penn Lady" from Frankford was discovered. A passionate advocate for Pennsylvania's founder, she had been pursuing bestowing honorary citizenship for William and Hannah Penn for many years. Vivian and Meyer Potamkin, art collectors, attended meetings and added their support. The committee welcomed everyone who could help advance their mission.*
>
> *Dr. Pettyjohn suggested that the committee be named the Penn Treaty Park Tercentenary Committee. This would connect the members to the upcoming events scheduled for the 300th anniversary of the Great Treaty and the founding of Pennsylvania in 1982.*

The consensus of the committee was to attempt to secure additional property adjacent to the existing park. Some of the land was vacant but an existing millwork company occupied one parcel. The committee was an eclectic collection of enthusiastic volunteers, but complete novices as to how to achieve this ambitious goal. We needed to learn the entire process: how to acquire the land, how to work with political representatives, how to develop a design, how to reach consensus in the community.

Elected officials and various government agencies were invited to meetings. We benefited from the youthful enthusiasm of Sandy Salzman, secretary of the Fishtown Civic Association, as well as President Jim Winn's advocacy. The efforts spanned nearly ten years, and during this time all the subsequent presidents of the Fishtown Civic Association supported the cause: Dot Sobotka, Carolyn O'Conner and Joe Torre.

Every agency, every person who could possibly impact the project was contacted. Councilman Jim Tayoun was a champion for having monies allocated for land acquisition and development. The efforts of Joe Torre and Councilman Tayoun were critical in navigating Philadelphia's bureaucracy. Henry Kreiss, "Mr. Kensington," a dignified elder statesman always attired in a suit and tie, used his influence to meet with anyone who would help purchase the land. He relentlessly and determinedly kept the project moving forward. Dr. Pettyjohn influenced the regular meetings of the Tercentenary Committee, by bringing order and organization to the proceedings. Her presence commanded respect. The former principal of Kensington High School was a pillar of strength. She was proud of her Fishtown roots, her degrees from the University of Pennsylvania, and a champion of Penn Treaty Park.

Monies were successfully budgeted for the land acquisition, but we needed to develop a plan that would envision the newly expanded parkland. Alley Friends Architects Al Johnson and Richard Stange were hired to gather community input and to formalize a plan. However, the committee reached an impasse. Should the new area have formal recreation areas like baseball fields or a boat ramp? The committee was very divided about the conflicting proposals and we started to lose focus. Beatrice Kirkbride offered the proposition that the land be established simply as open space; an area for visitors to fly a kite, have a picnic, or just enjoy the riverside ambience. She felt that this setting would reflect William Penn's philosophy of peace and be a lasting tribute to the historical nature of the park. The idea carried the day and another hurdle was surmounted.

The statue of William Penn that now occupies such a distinctive place in the park also became a part of the Committee's proceedings. In honor of the 300th anniversary of Pennsylvania, the National Society of the Daughters of the American Colonists, proposed to have a sculpture commissioned by Frank Gaylord. However the sculpture was rejected by the Art Commission and it appeared it would not be placed at the Park. Elaine Peden, the "William Penn lady" who was part of the Tercentenary Committee, knew the president of the Daughters, Mrs. Mary Foster. Mrs. Foster, from York, Pa., visited the site and concurred that it was an appropriate setting. With the encouragement of Elaine Peden, the complete support of the Tercentenary Committee and Councilman Tayoun, the Penn statue found a home in a prominent place in the park.

Over many years, the committee had extraordinary success in achieving its goals. It displayed the finest qualities of building community consensus, establishing partnerships with elected officials, working cooperatively with any interested group and bringing an ambitious vision to reality. Five acres of waterfront land was preserved because of the unselfish efforts and wide support from hundreds of people. Penn's spirit of friendship and good will prevailed throughout these efforts and today Penn Treaty Park is a peaceful oasis along the Delaware River, a place of gathering and community, just as it was in the time that Penn met with the Native Americans so long ago.

John Connors, Chairman Penn Treaty Park Tercentenary Committee 2007

Land north and south of the park was on the market for sale, and plans were struck by the Fishtown Civic Association to try to get the city to purchase land and expand the park. Efforts were then made to get the money in the capital budget so that the city would be able to purchase the ground. An endless stream of letters was sent to local congressmen, the Fairmount Park Commission, the City Planning Commission, the then-mayor William Green and many members of the city council, including Fishtown's councilman, James Tayoun. These letters were followed up by personal visits, with most of these visits conducted by Connors and his mentor "Mr. Kensington," Henry C. Kreiss. Kreiss and Connors even testified before city council in order to persuade the council to expand the park.

While Connors, Kreiss, et al., spearheaded the community's effort, committee member Joe Torre, as well as Councilman Jimmy Tayoun, spearheaded the political front. Tayoun stated in an interview that he had an easy enough time introducing legislation to council for the inclusion of monies in the city budget for surveying, planning and acquiring the land for the expansion of the park. There was no opposition from other council members, nor was there opposition

John Connors (left) and Henry C. Kriese, in his customary suit, were leaders in the neighborhood's expansion of Penn Treaty Park, 1987. *Courtesy John Connors Collection.*

Councilman James Tayoun flanked by Dr. Etta May Pettyjohn (right) and Caroline O'Connor, circa 1982. *Courtesy John Connors Collection.*

from the port authority or the chamber of commerce, to turn the waterfront commercial properties into parkland. He said he acted as the railroad to transport the community's wishes through the red tape roadblocks of government.

The only real problems that Tayoun faced were the time factors involved in having the process go through the bureaucracy that is Philadelphia city government. Every year monies had to be secured and put into the budget, and finally, after a number of years, the project was completed. Due to the time it took to get the necessary monies allocated, it was good that the tercentenary committee had the foresight to plan the expansion of the park years in advance, so that it might be completed on time for the 300th anniversary of the city of Philadelphia. While the landscaping of the expanded portion of the park was not completed in 1982, the land was nevertheless secured.

Two properties south of the park were identified for purchase by the City of Philadelphia. The Fairmount Park Commission identified these properties as 1201–1211 N. Delaware Avenue, owned by Warner Company, which specialized in storage and distribution of building materials but in 1979 was leasing the property as a lumber storage yard to Penn Atlantic Millworks, Inc. The second property was the rear of 1227–1237 Beach Street, which

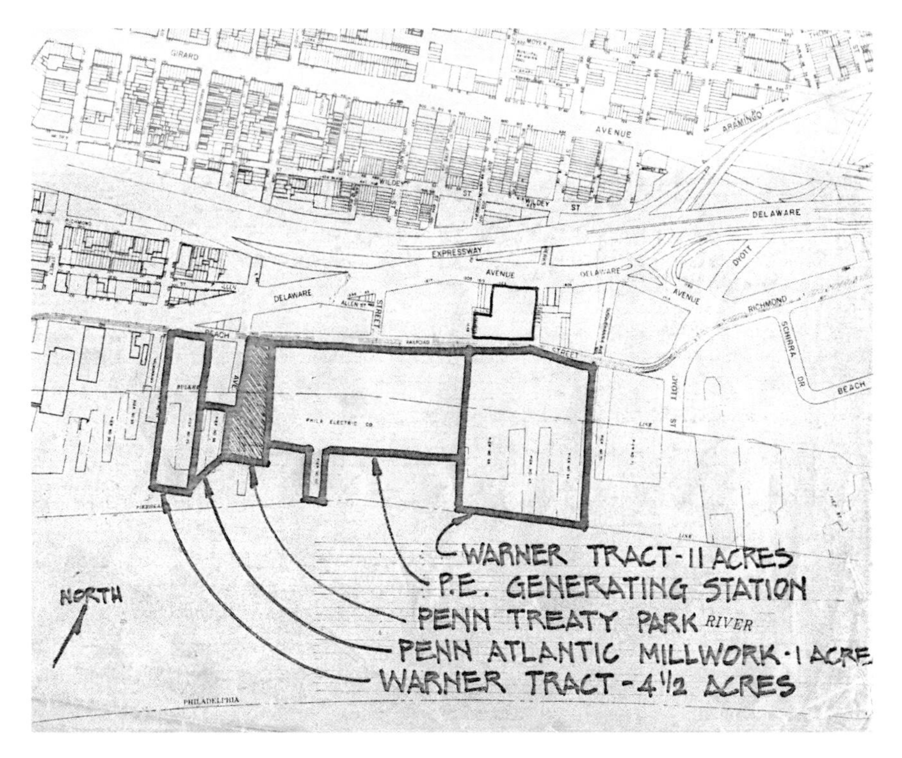

A map showing the land much discussed for purchase to be used for park expansion. Eventually the 4.5-acre Warner Tract south of the park was acquired, circa 1980. *Courtesy John Connors Collection.*

was owned by Penn Atlantic Millworks, Inc. The property housed several brick structures that housed mill shops and the remains of Pier 56.

With these tracts of land south of the park identified, efforts were made to acquire the land and expand the park from Columbia Avenue south to Marlborough Street. An ordinance (Bill No. 325, September 24, 1980) authorizing the commissioner of public property to purchase these properties to expand the park was approved and signed by Mayor William Green. The "Warner Tract" of about four acres was purchased in 1980 for a little over $151,000, and the "Penn Atlantic Millwork Tract" of one acre was purchased in 1983. It had been appraised at $48,600.

Now that the land was secured, all that was needed was to remove the structures on the properties. After the demolition of the warehouses and landscaping of the new five acres of expansion, the area would be incorporated into Penn Treaty Park.

Artist Troy Dalton installing his "Penn Treaty Park Expansion" sign in the soon-to-be-expanded parkland, circa 1981–82. *Courtesy John Connors Collection.*

Old warehouses and the Mobil Gas Station south of the park were demolished to make room for expansion, circa 1983–84. *Courtesy John Connors Collection.*

According to a report issued by the Fairmount Park Commission ("Penn Treaty Park: Growth and Evolution 2008"), the properties were covered with debris, abandoned railroad spurs and building materials. Additionally, both properties had badly deteriorated piers. The commission's engineers also needed to reconfigure the shoreline, which they did between November 1982 and July 1983. Hired contractors removed "portions of an old pier and filled a portion of a slip. Piers 54, 55, and 56 were dramatically reconfigured and rip rap was placed to protect the reconfigured shoreline." Columbia Avenue also needed to be stricken from the city plan.

The Fishtown Civic Association worked with Alley Friends Architects to get ideas for how to design the expanded park area. After much debate over what the park should and should not incorporate (sports fields, trees, fishing pier, etc.), Beatrice Kirkbride suggested leaving a grand open space. Her idea won out. The Fairmount Park Commission, working with Hexagon Architectural Group, Ltd., designed a large open space with several curved walkways, with a slightly inclined hill on the Beach Street side that would allow an open-air theatre–type setting in that area of the park. The large open field allowed for kite flying, Frisbee throwing, soccer playing and other

The expansion of the park in 1987 brought a new fishing pier. A tugboat crashed into the pier circa 2005, destroying the pier. *Courtesy John Connors Collection.*

outdoor activities. A small fishing pier was constructed about 1985–86, but an out-of-control tugboat crashed into the pier about five years ago, damaging it so badly that it needed to be removed. Apparently a settlement was made by the tugboat's insurance company, but the money was never used to repair or build another fishing pier; thus the park now has no fishing pier after having one for most of its existence. Safety issues (kids diving off into the river) were the usual reasons given for not building another pier.

Amazingly, at a time when the city was slashing its budget and when monies for already-existing parks were barely being maintained, Connors, Kreiss, et al., were able to secure a great deal of monies from the Fairmount Park Commission and the city government to purchase two tracts of land south of the park, demolish the existing structures on those properties, renovate and landscape a new five-acre expansion of the park.

In 1986–87, the 120th annual report was issued by the Fairmount Park Commission. This report mentions the work that composed the expansion of Penn Treaty Park. The commission provided "supervision and construction management for the creation of a complete recreational park adjacent to the original historic site, where William Penn is said to have signed his treaty with the Indians." The cost of building this new part of the park was $574,000,

The newly expanded park and its landscaped walkways offered a green space by the river for Fishtowners and Kensingtonians, circa 1992. *Courtesy John Connors Collection.*

The expanded park's shoreline. Kensington ME "Old Brick" Church, the oldest church in Kensington, is in the background at center, circa 1992. *Courtesy John Connors Collection.*

of which $270,000 came from the Federal Land and Water Conservation Fund. This fund was to expire in 1989. The Fairmount Park Commission used monies from this fund to the tune of $1.9 million since 1965 for land acquisition and rehabilitation.

On Sunday, November 1, 1987, Philadelphia city officials, the Fairmount Park Commission and members of the Fishtown Civic Association and the Kensington Community Council all came together with members of the community to help celebrate the official rededication of Penn Treaty Park. The Gaylord sculpture of Penn was in place on its new, enlarged base, and the park was expanded with the five acres previously acquired. New landscaping was complete and the fishing pier was in place. A slight incline on the western edge of the expanded park that fronted a large open space made for an open-air theatre setting on the Delaware River.

With the music of the police band and dancing by various troupes, the Penn Treaty Park welcomed dignitaries such as Philadelphia mayor W. Wilson Goode, Congressman Thomas M. Foglietta and State Senator Vincent Fumo, as well as members of Fishtown Civic Association, Kensington Community Council and Chief William Lynch of the United American Indians of Delaware Valley.

John J. Connors, chairman of the Penn Treaty Park Committee, dressed as a Quaker, participated in the reenactment of the landing of William Penn and his Treaty of Amity and Friendship with the Native Americans.

The rededication of the park in 1987 was a resounding success, and Fishtown now had one of the few open space public parks on the Delaware River within the city of Philadelphia.

On May 1, 1989, Chief Jake Swamp of the Mohawk Tribe and 150 people gathered at Penn Treaty Park and planted a small white pine tree. The project was organized by Toni Truesdale, a shop teacher and artist at Mastbaum Vo-Tech School in Kensington. The tree planting led off a four-day conference titled "Forgotten Legacy: Native American Concepts and the Formation of the United States." May 1 used to be known as "Tammany's Day," a celebration of the merging of the European and Indian cultures. Chief Tamanend was the one who made the treaty with William Penn.

The plaque on the "Direct Descendant Tree" was first ordered on October 6, 1998, and scheduled to be installed mid-April 1999. On June 7, 2000, a Fairmount Park ground crew planted an elm tree that was a descendant of the Treaty Elm. The "Great American Elm" that was planted that day replaced a similar one that did not survive after being planted earlier. That may have been the tree that the Fishtown Civic Association planted

Tercentenary committee chairman John Connors dressed in Quaker garb during the park celebrations, 1982. *Courtesy John Connors Collection.*

Overview of Penn Treaty Park. The group of trees on the right is the original park; to the left is the five-acre expansion. *Courtesy John Connors Collection.*

on October 24, 1982. They had acquired a sapling from the grandson of the Treaty Elm Tree that had been planted at Haverford College. This Haverford College tree was planted at the college in the 1840s; it was the son of a tree that General Paul A. Oliver, the husband of Mary Vandusen, had planted at his home in Bay Ridge, New York, but had later transplanted to Wilkes-Barre, Pennsylvania. Oliver's original tree came from a sapling of the original Treaty Elm when it was blown down in 1810. Mary Vandusen's family was the owner of the Treaty Elm land and Fairman's Mansion.

Later, in 2002, American Indians again visited Penn Treaty Park. As part of a 330-mile canoe trip to promote stewardship for the Delaware River, and promoting the history and perilous future of the Lenni-Lenape Indians, Native American Jim Beer and others arrived to rest and commemorate Penn Treaty Park. "The only ancient history of Pennsylvania is our people's history," said Beer, who lives in Upper Bucks County, Pennsylvania. "Preserving Lenape history is preserving the ancient history of Pennsylvania." Beer is a descendant of the Lenape, or Delaware Indians, the original inhabitants of the Delaware River Valley. A symbolic treaty was signed between the surviving Lenni-

Lenape Tribe and the Delaware River Greenway, a consortium of more than one hundred government agencies and nonprofit groups. The various groups, organizations and the Lenni-Lenape Indians have an interest in caring for and protecting the Delaware River Valley. While the treaty signing didn't take place at Penn Treaty Park (they signed it at Pennsbury Manor), the two groups did ensure that Penn Treaty Park was honored as part of their journey.

Friends of Penn Treaty Park

After the tercentenary celebrations in 1982 and the rededication of the expanded park in 1987, John Connors wrote on April 6, 1989, to the Fairmount Park Commission about creating a "Friends of the Park" organization. The first meeting of this new group was scheduled for April 17, 1989. The meeting was to be held at Peg's Dinner across from the park. On February 22, 1990, it was announced at the Friends of the Park meeting that elections were held and that Anna Marie Armstrong and Chris Schueler were elected co-chairs of the group. The recording secretary was Jamie Swanson, with Lynn Wigglesworth being elected corresponding secretary. Brian Helfrich was elected treasurer.

For one reason or another, the energy ran out and the Friends of the Park started to falter. However, as Fishtown entered a new chapter in its history, a great gentrification process came over the neighborhood, beginning in the late 1990s. With many new people moving into the community and many more becoming aware of Penn Treaty Park for the first time, the new energy helped to form a nucleus, and a combination of old-timers and newcomers were able to breathe life into the Friends of Penn Treaty Park and thus the group was reborn.

The first year of the rebirth of the group saw regular monthly cleanups, and the park looks spectacular on most days. New playground equipment was installed, and regular fundraisers have been conducted (such as "Champagne in the Park") that are proving to be highly successful, not only to raise funds for the park, but also to help neighbors get to know each other. Recently a large grant has been pledged that will allow the Friends to work with architects to help design plans for the park's future.

The history of Penn Treaty Park continues one person at a time, as public-spirited citizens add their chapter to the park's history. Become a part of the history and contact the Friends of the Park. For more information, visit the Friends of Penn Treaty Park's website: www.penntreatypark.org.

CHAPTER 6

THE ARTWORK IN THE PARK

Each of the three pieces of artwork in Penn Treaty Park has its own interesting story of how it came to be placed in the park. The "trio of artwork," as they are called, took great effort to acquire, much like the founding of the park itself. Each of the three pieces of artwork has much to say about the park, the community, the local government and how the local community has worked with and fought with the local government to preserve, honor and care for Penn Treaty Park.

The Penn Treaty Monument

The background history of the Penn Treaty Memorial, the original obelisk monument to Penn's Treaty, has already been mentioned in the second chapter. The Penn Society placed the monument at the site of the Treaty Elm Tree in 1827. At that time, the land was in private hands, and the Penn Society never acquired an easement from the owners of the property; thus, the monument sat on private property with the permission of the owner of the lot. Over time, as the area became much more developed and the land more expensive, the beginnings of the movement for the creation of Penn Treaty Park took place, and the park was eventually founded in 1893 with the monument still sitting in its original location at the northwest corner of the park.

Treaty Ground of William Penn and the Indian Natives 1682 Unbroken Faith, original monument created by the Penn Society in 1827. *Courtesy John Connors Collection.*

Obelisk monument in its original spot, the northwest corner of Penn Treaty Park, placed there by the Penn Society in 1827, circa 1954. *Courtesy Philadelphia City Archives.*

The location of the treaty monument has always played a role in the history of the piece. While the monument was placed to honor and remind people of Penn's Treaty, it was never located on the exact spot of the Treaty Elm Tree, as some have proposed. It was placed in the northwest corner so it would be out of the way of any business conducted on the grounds of the old lumberyard that once stood at that spot. Because of this fact—that it did not mark the exact spot of the Treaty Elm—it allowed a later generation to move the obelisk to another location as the park was renovated and redesigned.

It is said that the famed architect John Haviland created the original obelisk that was designed for the Penn Society and that it was shown at one of the meetings of that group. It was decided then that it was too costly for the newly formed society to erect, and thus a simpler model was substituted for it.

The obelisk measures about five feet nine inches tall and was placed on the grounds of the Penn Treaty Wharf, near the spot where the Treaty Tree once stood. Presumably, the men placing the monument in 1827 would have

Another view of the obelisk monument, facing east, after the park was transferred to the Fairmount Park Commission, circa 1954. *Courtesy Philadelphia City Archives.*

known exactly where the tree stood as they were all living when the tree blew down seventeen years previously, but they needed to place the monument in the corner of the lot so that it was out of the way of business, as mentioned.

The four sides of the obelisk have the following inscriptions (by the compass—north, south, east and west):

Treaty ground of William Penn, and the Indian Nations, 1682, Unbroken faith.

William Penn, Born 1644, Died 1713.

Pennsylvania, Founded, 1681, by Deeds of Peace.

Placed by the Penn Society, A.D. 1827, to mark the site of the Great Elm Tree.

At some point, an iron fence was erected around the monument, but this must have been some years after the obelisk was placed as there are early reports of lumber being piled up around the monument and the monument being obscured from sight. In December 1880, local councilman Benjamin Faunce introduced a resolution in council to acquire some of the fencing being taken down in Washington Square to be recycled and used for the fencing in of the Penn Treaty Monument.

When the Philadelphia Electric Company built its generating plant on the north side of Penn Treaty Park, it took down the old brick wall that served as the backdrop for the treaty monument for many years. In its place, PECO built an iron fence between its property and the park. It was about this time that the background of the treaty monument also changed. The brick wall was gone and replaced by a much nicer and fancier white stone wall. The rest of the property line between PECO and the park had the iron fence. It's unclear who paid for the new background of the monument.

A Fairmount Park Commission plan of the park dated June 7, 1971, shows the treaty monument still located in the northwest corner. From the PECO property line going south along the pavement edge of the park on Beach Street, the plot measured roughly an 18-feet-square plot, surrounded with an iron fence. The center of the actual obelisk itself sat 5.6 feet south from the PECO property line and 16.9 feet from the curb of Beach Street.

Some believe that the treaty monument was moved during renovations for the bicentennial in 1976; however, a photograph dated November 21, 1978, at the Fairmount Park Historic Resource Archive shows the monument still at the northwest corner location. The plaque that was placed on the present pedestal that surrounds the monument where it is located today was approved on May 31, 1978; thus, the monument must have been moved from its original location soon after the November 1978 photograph—perhaps the reason why the monument was being photographed by the commission. Further proof for the monument being moved in later 1978 or soon after is provided in the Fairmount Park Commission's annual report for 1977–78, which stated that "this historic park is being rehabilitated, including new walkways, sitting areas, fencing, lighting, landscaping, and relocation of monument."

During the discussions of moving the treaty monument from its original location to where it sits today, local historian George Baker and his friend William Wright disagreed with the movement. Wright, in a letter to Baker dated October 1, 1976, told Baker that he thought moving the monument to the middle of the park was plain wrong. Baker wrote to Robert C. McConnell, the director of the Fairmount Park Commission, on February 24, 1977, and asked McConnell to have the commission research Wright's assertion that the center of the park was not the appropriate place to move the monument. On January 18, 1977, in a previous letter to McConnell, Baker wrote that he disagreed with the commission's decision to move the monument and told him that the new location would actually be three feet into the Delaware River if the area had not been built up over the years with landfill. McConnell, in a return letter to Baker, disagreed and stated that since the original placement of the monument did not mark the exact spot of the Treaty Tree, it did not matter where the monument was moved to as the new placement of the monument would still be within sixty to seventy feet of the original Treaty Elm and within the span of the tree's limbs.

Since the commission cited Charles J. Lukens's article from *Sloan's Architectural Review & Builder's Journal* of 1868 in an application to the National Register of Historic Places, and since that article by Lukens pointed out (with a map) the original site of the Treaty Tree, it would appear that the exact location of the Treaty Elm was not important to the commission—their new design of the park would take precedence over the park's history and tradition, thus an opportunity for marking the exact spot of the Treaty Elm was lost. The paperwork on this battle over the movement of the treaty monument between local historians of Fishtown and the Fairmount Park Commission shows that the commission hired Asplund, an environmental services company, to do the research for the history of the location of the Treaty Elm.

The original obelisk monument after it was moved (circa 1979) to its current resting place. *Courtesy Karen Mauch Photography © 2008.*

After the treaty monument was moved, Matthews Architectural Division designed the plaque mentioned above, which is forty-eight by thirty-two inches by three-fourths of an inch and is made of aluminum with a metallic finish. The lettering on the plaque was made in a Helvetica-type font with the wording as follows:

While other colonies were in conflict and in great distress
with the Indians, William Penn, through his philosophy of
social justice and peace, engaged their friendship and goodwill.

Here is the site of the Great Treaty of Amity between
William Penn and the Indians, which was held in November 1682,
for the purpose of establishing a permanent friendship.
The Treaty is thought to have been held under the Great
Elm Tree, which was blown down by heavy winds on Saturday
Night, March 3, 1810 [actually March 5].

The leaves of the seal represents The Great Elm, and the
Wampum Belt represents the Great Treaty of Amity.

THE DAC, FRANK C. GAYLORD AND THE WILLIAM PENN SCULPTURE

The Daughters of the American Colonists (DAC) is a national society with approximately eleven thousand members from all over America. Membership to the DAC is offered to any woman of eighteen years or older, of good moral character and who can trace her lineage to an ancestor who rendered civil or military service in any of the colonies prior to American Independence (July 4, 1776).

The DAC was founded in 1923 as a society of women whose objects were patriotic, historical and educational. According to the DAC's website, the society "researches the history and deeds of American colonists to record and publish them; to commemorate deeds of colonial interest; to inculcate and foster a love of the United States of America and its institutions by all its residents; and to obey its laws and venerate its flag."

The DAC's objectives are carried out by its many committees:

> *Flags of the United States of America Committee; the National Defense Committee; the Patriotic Education Committee, which works through schools and Naturalization Courts; the Veterans' Services Committee which, among other activities, encourages volunteer service in veterans hospitals; and the National Awards Committee, which provides annual gifts for achievement at the United States Service Academies across the country.*

There are also state societies and local chapters that present ROTC, American history and citizenship awards through the work of the National Awards Committee.

The historical work of the DAC is carried out through their Colonial and Genealogical Records Committee, which helps to preserve original records and researches and determines membership eligibilities, and through the Historic Landmarks and Memorials Committee that is responsible for helping to locate and mark sites of historical interest. There are also several other committees involved in commemorating various historical events and activities.

Each national president takes on the responsibility of a special project, the purpose being to enhance the objectives of the society. In 1980, during the presidency of Mrs. Mary Helen Foster, she wanted to present to the city of Philadelphia on its 300th anniversary a sculpture of William Penn. Mrs.

Eight-ton block of Barre granite from the Rock of Ages Quarry, from which the William Penn figure was sculpted by Frank C. Gaylord, circa 1981. *Courtesy John Connors Collection.*

Foster was familiar with the work of Frank C. Gaylord and contracted him to sculpt a figure of William Penn.

Frank C. Gaylord kept his sculpture studio in Barre, Vermont, the granite capital of America, and since Mrs. Foster wanted a sculpture in Vermont granite, the match with Gaylord was perfect. Gaylord would later gain further fame as the artist who sculpted the Korean War Memorial in Washington, D.C.

In a letter dated December 13, 1980, Gaylord stated that the cost of the sculpture would be $28,780 for a 7'6" figure and a 4' pedestal to be placed in the park by April 1982. An alternative price was $22,847 for a 6'6" figure and a 3'6" pedestal. The DAC decided on the smaller figure.

Work on the sculpture was to be done during 1981 and early 1982. The sculpture was made from an eight-ton block of Barre granite from the Rock of Ages Quarry. The block measured eight feet six inches by four feet by two feet six inches. It was first sent to a saw plant, where it was dimensioned. Large amounts of stone were removed using pneumatic drills. Smaller pneumatic drills were then used to shape the figure in rough form. Reference points on the model were located on the stone figure, and large planes were

The Daughters of the American Colonists (DAC) visit sculptor Frank C. Gaylord at his studio during creation of the William Penn figure, circa 1981. *Courtesy John Connors Collection.*

established on the figure. The planes were then broken into specific detail with a pneumatic chisel.

The Fairmount Park Commission declined the DAC's gift of Frank Gaylord's sculpture. The reason was said to be on the basis of aesthetic quality. However, Frankford's Elaine Peden, known throughout Pennsylvania as "the William Penn Lady," had other thoughts on the Fairmount Park Commission's decision. Peden had previously gained famed as being the person responsible for persuading the United States Congress to extend honorary citizenship upon William Penn and his wife Hannah Callowhill. She took a great interest in anything William Penn, and upon reading in a local paper of the Fairmount Park Commission's rejection of the William Penn figure, she immediately went into action to change that outcome.

According to Peden, Joe Brown, a member of the Fairmount Park Commission's art jury that rejected Gaylord's Penn sculpture, should have excused himself from the decision. Brown, a professional boxer turned sculptor, served as a boxing instructor at Princeton University, where he also lectured on creative arts. Peden believed that there was a conflict of interest on Brown's part, because Brown was eager to acquire the commission for the DAC's William Penn sculpture. There was one problem, though, and that

Frank C. Gaylord admiring his work. He later went on to create the Korean War Memorial at Washington, D.C., circa 1981–82. *Courtesy John Connors Collection.*

was the DAC's president Foster already had her sculptor, Frank C. Gaylord. Since Brown wanted to do the sculpture in bronze and Foster wanted it done in granite, Foster did not even bother to offer the commission to Brown. The jury, with Brown as one of its members, wound up voting against the acceptance of the Gaylord sculpture. Brown was more known for sculptures of sports figures. In 1976, four of his sports figures were placed at the old Veterans Stadium in South Philadelphia. He is also the person responsible for the goofy sculpture of Benjamin Franklin that sits on the west side of Broad Street, south of city hall and opposite the Masonic Temple.

After reading that the Fairmount Park Commission declined the sculpture of Penn, Elaine Peden talked with Mary Helen Foster. The two women hit it off right away and became lifelong friends. Peden was sure that together they could get the William Penn sculpture placed in Penn Treaty Park. Mrs. Foster's offer of the William Penn sculpture had only one condition on it—that it be placed in Penn Treaty Park.

When it became known that the Fairmount Park Commission declined the sculpture, other offers came in for placing the Gaylord sculpture in places in Philadelphia out of the reach of the Fairmount Park Commission. The

Elaine Peden, "the William Penn Lady," gives Gaylord's William Penn sculpture a big hug at the unveiling ceremonies, April 1982. *Courtesy John Connors Collection.*

The William Penn sculpture today, having been moved to the enlarged base at the rededication ceremonies for the expanded park in 1987. *Courtesy John Connors Collection.*

Community College of Philadelphia was one such institution that offered to take the sculpture of Penn for its rotunda in the Old Mint Building on Spring Garden Street. While Mrs. Foster listened attentively to the offer of the college, her heart was set on Penn Treaty Park. If the statue could not be placed in the park, it would be placed in her hometown of York, Pennsylvania.

Elaine Peden, like Mrs. Foster, thought there was no better place for the Penn figure than Penn Treaty Park. Peden contacted the Fishtown Civic Association and advised them that it was about to lose a valuable sculpture for Penn Treaty Park. Peden met with the Fishtown Civic and the DAC's president Foster, and the offer to the Fishtown Civic Association was an easy sell, with the civic group immediately getting behind the effort to place the sculpture in the park.

Back in 1979, the Fishtown Civic Association formed the Penn Treaty Park Tercentenary Committee. The committee included not only members of the Fishtown Civic Association, but also members of the Fishtown Athletic Club, the American Society of Friends, the Kensington Community Council, former residents and other interested parties. The chairman of this committee was none other than John Connors, an active Penn Treaty Park booster and spirited citizen. Besides planning celebrations for Pennsylvania's 300th anniversary, the tercentenary committee was also successful in getting PECO to shield its transformers at Beach Street and Columbia Avenue by building a brick wall and convincing Congressman Ray Lederer to try to get national landmark status for Penn Treaty Park.

When Elaine Peden contacted the Fishtown Civic Association about the possibility of Penn Treaty Park being the resting place for Gaylord's sculpture, the civic group and the tercentenary committee were ecstatic.

In early 1981, the Fairmount Park Commission, with the prodding of the Fishtown Civic and "the William Penn Lady," and perhaps some local political pressure, finally committed to accepting the Gaylord sculpture for Penn Treaty Park, provided the Fairmount Park Art Commission approved, which it did.

The William Penn statue was placed in the park on April 22, 1982. The dedication ceremony for the unveiling of the sculpture took place two days later on April 24, 1982. The unveiling was part of the opening events for the "Century IV Celebration," the 300th anniversary of Pennsylvania.

Within a month of the sculpture of Penn being placed in the park, the figure was vandalized with spray-painted graffiti. Actions were taken by the Fishtown Civic Association, and letters written to the Fairmount Park Commission and to the sculptor Frank Gaylord. All agreed that the sculpture should be cleaned and treated with an anti-graffiti solution. Gaylord even thought that the solution would enhance the piece.

BOB HAOZOUS AND THE PENN TREATY SCULPTURE

Between 1987 and 1988, the City of Philadelphia purchased the triangular piece of land that sits between Beach Street and Delaware Avenue, south of Columbia Avenue, called 1227–1233 N. Delaware Avenue. The price for the property was $131,836. When the city first looked at the property in 1979, it was appraised at $48,600. A Mobil Gas Station sat on southern part of the triangular corner of the property, with the northern portion having a two-story brick warehouse. Today this strip of land is the home of Bob Haozous's metal plate sculpture, *Penn Treaty*. The story of how Penn Treaty Park became the home of Haozous's sculpture demonstrates another troubled chapter of Penn Treaty Park's history.

Penn Treaty Park's bicentennial celebrations passed in 1976, and the state's tercentennial celebrations passed in 1982. The newly expanded part of the park was not yet landscaped in 1982, and thus more work was needed

Ron Anderson's Stonehenge-like creation was one of the four finalists for the Indian sculpture complement to the park, 1988. *Courtesy Fairmount Park Historic Resource Archive.*

Karl Cieslak, one of the four finalists for the Indian sculpture complement, created this fountain-like sculpture, 1988. *Courtesy Fairmount Park Historic Resource Archive.*

to prepare the park. By 1987, with everything now in order and the newly expanded park in tiptop shape, the Penn Treaty Park rededication was held on Sunday, November 1, 1987.

At a meeting of the Fairmount Park Commission later that month (November 23, 1987), the commission discussed adding a third piece of artwork to the park. The third piece would be dedicated to Native Americans. The piece would complement the other two pieces of artwork in the park, the Gaylord sculpture of Penn and the original Penn Treaty Monument, to form a trio of artwork.

The commission set about creating a national competition with a budget of $50,000. Thousands of notices were sent out to artists throughout America and Canada, with about one hundred artists responding. The notice stated that the artwork would be a"traditional" piece that would complement the other two pieces of artwork in the park. The jury that was formed for the competition reviewed the proposals and in time narrowed the field down. On June 13, 1988, the advisory committee for the Penn Treaty Artwork Competition met to review the four finalists: Ron Anderson, Phoenix, Arizona; Bob Haozous, Sante Fe, New Mexico; Karl Cieslak, Ottawa, Ontario, Canada; and Joyce De Guatemala, Glenmore, Pennsylvania.

Ron Anderson was a minimalist who created a piece resembling the famous Stonehenge monument in England. It was made up of thirteen slabs of stone standing up on end. It was difficult to see the relationship of Anderson's Stonehenge-like work with Penn's Treaty.

Karl Cieslak's piece was a circular-based fountain, with a large stone in the center and a disc-like piece sticking out of it, surrounded by a circular brick walkway. Like Anderson's piece, this piece also seemed out of place for Penn Treaty Park.

Joyce De Guatemala came up with an idea of a sculpture using the wampum belt figure images of William Penn and Tamanend. She placed them within a tube-like platform on a circular bed raised slightly above the ground with a stone border, surrounded by a brick paved walk. De Guatemala previously had a commission for the ten-foot-high stainless steel sculpture that sits outside the front doors of the Elkins Park Free Library. De Guatemala is a Mexican artist who works primarily with planes of stainless steel with origins in the concepts of art and architecture found in Mayan archaeology integrated into contemporary technology.

Bob Haozous created a large double metal plate sculpture and also used the wampum belt figure motifs, along with symbols of airplanes and clouds. At the time of the competition, Haozous was working in heavy plate steel and with symbols of puffy clouds and airplanes that represented pollution,

Joyce De Guatemala, another of the four finalists, created a piece using the wampum belt figures, 1988. *Courtesy Fairmount Park Historic Resource Archive.*

modernization and technology. The double heavy steel plates of his sculpture show a positive-negative transposition—the rear plate is covered with puffy clouds and the front plate has an image of William Penn and an American Indian that was inspired by the famous wampum belt given to Penn by the Native Americans. As you walk around the sculpture, the scene constantly changes because of the cutouts in the steel, as well as the positive-negative transposition of the two back-to-back plates.

The four finalists prepared models, which went on exhibit at the Atwater Kent Museum between October 1 and October 16, 1988, with the selection of the winner to be made on October 17 and presented to the Fairmount Park Art Commission at its November 1988 meeting.

During the exhibition, the commission took written comments on what viewers thought of the work of the four finalists. As recorded, the exhibition comments were mostly negative for all four pieces. Some commentators simply wanted the artists to include more of the philosophy behind the work, others thought the works were unclear and still others thought that some

Bob Haozous (born 1945) originally wanted his *Penn Treaty* sculpture placed farther inside the park near the river. *Courtesy Karen Mauch Photography © 2008.*

were a downright disgrace. Locally, longtime Penn Treaty Park advocates were mostly against the four projects. James Weiss and Elaine Peden "wanted an Indian." The late Dr. Etta May Pettyjohn thought that if one of the four pieces were to be mandated, she would have to choose Karl Cieslak's piece. Sandy Salzman wanted more information on what the works were supposed to represent. Carol Smythe's comment was a simple question mark ("?"). A local sculptor working in Philadelphia thought his graduate students did much better work and called the four finalists an "absurd disaster." He also called into question the committee who selected the finalists and thought that they should also take responsibility.

Local residents were not alone in their dismay of the finalists. Thomas Kline, chief engineer for the Fairmount Park Commission, also called into question the work of the four finalists. In a letter dated April 4, 1989, Kline was miffed by what he thought was a poor selection process by the jury and thought the whole process should be redone. The plans for the park had called for "traditional" artwork to compliment Gaylord's sculpture of Penn and the Penn Treaty Monument. All four finalists had created "contemporary" artwork models.

Bob Haozous was nevertheless selected as the winner of the competition. His piece utilized elements of the wampum belt. Haozous visited Philadelphia to view the wampum belt and liked how the beaded matrix of the belt gave the appearance of a digital image, and for this reason the images of Penn and the Native American from the wampum belt were incorporated into the sculpture. The figures of Penn and a Native American symbolized the encounter between European and Native American cultures, as well as commemorating the treaty itself. The wampum belt was the only object that has survived that represents the treaty. Against the wampum belt figures, Haozous played with symbols of nature and modern technology (clouds and airplanes) to give us the historic images of the treaty and the modern world.

The major element of the sculpture was cut welded steel, two plates measuring eight by twelve feet, mounted vertically six inches apart, parallel to each other. The base at the top was ten by three feet, tapering down to twelve by five feet. The weight of the sculpture was upwards of twelve thousand pounds.

Haozous was awarded a commission on October 18, 1988; however, by June 28, 1989, he still did not have his contract. Part of the problem was that there was hardly any support for the piece. The Fishtown Civic Association, while not liking the piece and not wanting the sculpture to be placed in the

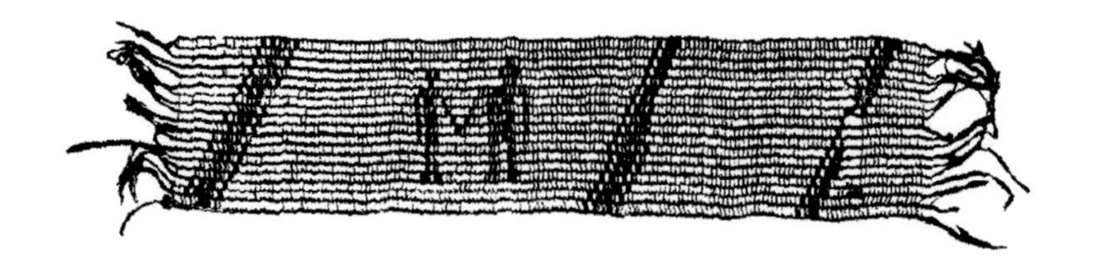

The wampum belt figure images were also used by Bob Haozous to create his winning welded-steel sculpture for Penn Treaty Park. *Courtesy John Connors Collection.*

park, was alarmed that the process was moving so slowly. Members were afraid that the grant money would be lost for the project if not spent that fiscal year.

With the community not liking Haozous's winning sculpture and some of its own members not wanting the piece, the Fairmount Park Commission had a real problem on its hands. In order to iron out the details of the contract and mitigate the concerns of the Fairmount Park Commission, Haozous was eventually forced to hire the Pittsburgh law firm of Costello, Yablonski, Leckie, Chaban. Other than nobody wanting the sculpture, there were a number of other issues slowing the process—questions related to insurance for the production, transportation and installation of the piece, various liabilities after the piece was installed, safety features and on what sort of base the sculpture would be placed.

Haozous, in a letter to William Mifflin, the executive director of the Fairmount Park Commission, stated that the base of the sculpture should be high enough to discourage climbing. It would be metal or concrete. A ten-foot-high base would be sufficient, and the planting of thorny shrubs around the piece would also help to discourage vandals and climbers. The rusted steel appearance of the piece would also make it easily maintainable—if it was graffitied one would only have to sandblast it and let it rust again. Haozous also felt that the rusted metal appearance fit into the industrial landscape of the area.

Finally, on July 2, 1991, the Fairmount Park Commission and Bob Haozous signed a contract. While the budget was originally set at $50,000, it was raised to $55,000, with a transportation cost of up to $4,000, bringing the total cost to $59,000.

Originally, the park's new renovation plans called for the Indian sculpture to be located on "Indian Island," a circular plot of ground located within the park, and acting as the third point of a triangle with the other two pieces of artwork (the Penn statue and the obelisk), with Indian Island being located southeast of the other two pieces. However, Haozous felt that his sculpture would fit better at the river's edge, south of the new fishing pier (now gone). This would enable the piece to be viewed by river traffic as well as people in the park, and since the original competition rules stated that the piece needed to be seen from land and sea, it seemed like a good placement to Haozous. However, with neighbors not wanting the sculpture in the park, the Fairmount Park Commission was in a bind. When all was said and done, the sculpture wound up outside the park on a small island between Beach Street and Delaware Avenue, south of Columbia Avenue, on a strip of land owned by the commission. The sculpture tends not to stand out but to blend in with the industrial landscape, looking more like a vacant iron billboard than a prized piece of artwork.

FURTHER READING

Clarkson, Thomas. *Memoirs of the Private and Public Life of William Penn. In Two Volumes in One.* London: Longman, Hurst, Rees, Orme and Brown, 1813.

Dunn, Mary Maples, Richard S. Dunn and Edwin B. Bronner, eds. *The Papers of William Penn.* 5 vols. Philadelphia: University of Pennsylvania Press, 1981–87.

Dunn, Richard S., and Mary Maples Dunn, eds. *The World of William Penn.* Philadelphia: University of Pennsylvania Press, 1986.

Du Ponceau, Pierre S., and J. Francis Fisher. *A Memoir on the History of the Celebrated Treaty made by William Penn with the Indians: Under the Elm Tree at Shackamaxon, in the Year 1682.* Found in *Memoirs of the Historical Society of Pennsylvania.* Vol. III, part II. Philadelphia: McCarty and Davis, 1836.

Endy, Melvin B., Jr. *William Penn and Early Quakerism.* Princeton, NJ: Princeton University Press, 1973.

Fanelli, Doris Devine, and Karie Diethorn. *History of the Portrait Collection, Independence National Historical Park.* Upper Darby, PA: Diane Publishing, 2001.

Heckewelder, John, and Pierre S. du Ponceau. *An account of the history, manners and customs of the Indian nations who once inhabited Pennsylvania and the neighbouring states: A correspondence between the Rev. John Heckewelder…and Pierre S. Duponceau…respecting the languages of the American Indians; Words, phrases and short dialogues in the language of the Lenni Lenape or Delaware Indians*. Found in *Transactions of the Historical & Literary Committee of the American Philosophical Society*. Vol. I. Philadelphia: A. Small, 1819.

Keyser, Charles S. *Penn's Treaty with the Indians*. Philadelphia: David McKay, 1882.

Myers, Albert Cook, ed. *William Penn's own account of the Lenni Lenape or Delaware Indians. 1683. Rev. Ed. Edited, and with an Introduction by Albert Cook Myers*. Somerset, NJ: Middle Atlantic Press, 1970.

Oldmixon, John. *The British Empire in America, containing the history of the discovery, settlement, progress and present state of all the British colonies on the continent and islands of America*. 2 vols. London: J. Nicholson, B. Tooke, 1708.

Peare, Catherine Owens. *William Penn: a Biography*. Philadelphia: Lippincott, 1956.

Proud, Robert. *The History of Pennsylvania, in North America, from the original institution and settlement of that province, under the first proprietor and governor, William Penn, in 1681, till after the year 1742*. Philadelphia: Zachariah Poulson Jr., 1797–98.

Scharf, J. Thomas, and Thompson Westcott. *History of Philadelphia, 1609–1884*. 3 vols. Philadelphia: L.H. Everts & Company, 1884.

Stone, Frederick D. "Penn's Treaty With the Indians. Did it Take Place in 1682 or 1683?" *Pennsylvania Magazine of History and Biography* 6 (1882).

Vaux, Roberts. *A Memoir on the Locality of the Great Treaty between William Penn and the Indian Natives in 1682, Read before the Historical Society of Pennsylvania, September 19th, 1825*. Found in *Memoirs of the Historical Society of Pennsylvania*. Vol. I. Philadelphia: McCarty and Davis, 1826.

Watson, John Fanning. *Annals of Philadelphia, and Pennsylvania, in the Olden Time; Being a Collection of Memoirs, Anecdotes, and Incidents of the City and its Inhabitants, and of the Earliest Settlements of the Inland Part of Pennsylvania. Enlarged, with Many Revisions and Additions by Willis P. Hazard. Profusely Illustrated in Three Volumes.* Philadelphia: J.M. Stoddart & Company, 1879.

———. *The Indian Treaty for the Lands now the Site of Philadelphia and the Adjacent Country.* Found in *Memoirs of the Historical Society of Pennsylvania.* Vol. III, part II. Philadelphia: McCarty and Davis, 1836.

Weslager, C.A. *The Delaware Indians.* New Brunswick, NJ: Rutgers University Press, 1990.